"What a beautiful book! Grant weaves profound knowledge of scripture and doctrine to think theologically and spiritually in a terrible circumstance: his son's cancer treatment. The pediatric oncology ward becomes a deep place to discover God, for 'a God who can't be found in suffering can't be found anywhere.' No one will read this book without being enriched by Good News. I will return to this book very often."

—PAUL STROBLE
Retired Adjunct Professor, Eden Theological Seminary

"*Bone of My Bone* is a heartfelt emotional narrative about a father seeking spiritual understanding following his young son's cancer diagnosis. The author, a pastor, shares his insights and reflections during this challenging time, inviting readers to engage in a deeper conversation about their own experiences and to explore the question of where God is during unimaginable circumstances. This book is a poignant, vulnerable, and thought-provoking story that is a must-read."

—JAMI CURLEY
Dean of the College of Nursing and Social Sciences, Lourdes University

"In *Bone of my Bone*, Grant Romoser-Claunch has brought the work of theology out of the abstract world of ideas and into the living, breathing, and suffering world of a pediatric cancer ward. Eschewing easy answers or trite solutions, Romoser-Claunch is the be praised not only for his theological acumen but even more so for his hard-won human sensitivities that make this work achingly powerful. I commend this book to all who may wonder what theology is really for in a world that all too often turns away from the pain that lies at its heart."

—ADAM PLOYD
Dean, Davenport College, Yale University

"At once a stirring memoir of parenthood in crisis, a theological interrogation of suffering and pain, and a pastoral offering of a family's journey with pediatric cancer, Grant Romoser-Claunch has written a book that can guide, challenge, and comfort readers on various levels. *Bone of My Bone* boldly advances theological inquiry into the challenging subject of theodicy, even as it pulls no punches in sharing the agonizing personal experience of a pastor and his family. Honest, brave, and beautiful, this book tells a powerful story of suffering and hope and forges new important insights in Christian theology and pastoral care."

—DEBORAH KRAUSE
President, Eden Theological Seminary

Bone of My Bone

Bone of My Bone

Reflections from an Oncology Ward

GRANT ROMOSER-CLAUNCH

WIPF & STOCK · Eugene, Oregon

BONE OF MY BONE
Reflections from an Oncology Ward

Copyright © 2025 Grant Romoser-Claunch. All rights reserved. Except for brief quotations in critical publications or reviews, no part of this book may be reproduced in any manner without prior written permission from the publisher. Write: Permissions, Wipf and Stock Publishers, 199 W. 8th Ave., Suite 3, Eugene, OR 97401.

Wipf & Stock
An Imprint of Wipf and Stock Publishers
199 W. 8th Ave., Suite 3
Eugene, OR 97401

www.wipfandstock.com

PAPERBACK ISBN: 979-8-3852-4902-2
HARDCOVER ISBN: 979-8-3852-4903-9
EBOOK ISBN: 979-8-3852-4904-6

VERSION NUMBER 08/05/25

All Scripture quotations, unless otherwise indicated, are taken from the Holy Bible, New International Version®, NIV.® Copyright ©1973, 1978, 1984, 2011 by Biblica, Inc.™ Used by permission of Zondervan. All rights reserved worldwide. www.zondervan.com. The "NIV" and "New International Version" are trademarks registered in the United States Patent and Trademark Office by Biblica, Inc.™

Scripture quotations marked (NLT) are taken from the Holy Bible, New Living Translation, copyright ©1996, 2004, 2015 by Tyndale House Foundation. Used by permission of Tyndale House Publishers, Carol Stream, Illinois 60188. All rights reserved.

Scripture quotations marked (NRSVue) are taken from the New Revised Standard Version Updated Edition. Copyright © 2021 National Council of Churches of Christ in the United States of America. Used by permission. All rights reserved worldwide.

Dedication

I write this for my superhero, for my sweet Simon. You are—and radiate—joy and vitality and enthusiasm for the fullness of life. The world is better because you are in it. I dedicate this also to my wife Mikhaela, who is my rock, my grounding, my safe harbor, and my best friend. Your tenderness and faith have led me and carried me even when I didn't have any of my own. This book is also for Jack, our second baby, who is abundant and inexpressible light and grace and bliss. You are a daily reminder of sublime goodness and of the holiness of getting to rewrite our narratives. It is the greatest gift and joy of my life to be a family with you all.

This is for all of our friends who have battled against pediatric cancer, for our friends who parent and nurture them, and for our beloved nurses and doctors. I hope this writing honors you all. I hope you can read it and feel seen. I hope the God who is found in the quiet places brings you abundant light, life, and love. May he bless you and keep you always. You are doing a wonderful job. I'm so proud of you, and I'm so thankful for you.

Contents

Introduction | ix

Mariology | 1

Pneumatology | 36

Christology | 60

Salvation | 79

Miracles | 95

Prayer | 110

Eschatology | 119

Bibliography | 121

Introduction

Our wounds are our opening to the world.

THIS BOOK—THE WRITING PROCESS and the finished product—are deeply personal. It is a more vulnerable and more existentially necessary journey than anything I've ever embarked upon. These reflections don't come from the starting line of theory or abstraction but from my soul, shaped by my experiences of my son's diagnosis and time spent on an oncology floor. They are not just words. They are my life. They are an honest reckoning with trust in God, beliefs and assumptions about God, and what it means to be mortal. This is not a theodicy. It is a theology of suffering; a theology of hope; a theology of everyday life.

On some days I wasn't sure if I believed God existed. Most days I wasn't sure if I could trust God anymore. Likely not something you would want to hear your pastor say. I knew that, for me, this meant I had to do the hard work of reflecting and seeing what made sense with the God revealed in Christ Jesus and what doesn't—to put everything on the table.

However brief these reflections and their scope might be, they are mine and they are of incalculable gravity. The wrestling that is on these pages—much of which I didn't realize I believed until I started writing—I hope can be received as the truth of what they are. I go forward believing as Franciscan Richard Rohr teaches: you have to begin with the particular in order to ever get

Introduction

a good picture of the universal.[1] This is my personal story and individual perspective. From my particular experiences with the light of the horrors and beauty that can be found in the journey of pediatric cancer, I hope to explore the nature of God through classical Christian doctrines. If the truths of God cannot be found on a pediatric oncology floor then they do not exist at all.

I started writing as a form of therapy and processing. While in the bone marrow unit it was a daily urging from something within: a soul-deep restless energy. Eventually I started writing due to the mixture of the constant internal nagging and because I could feel in my body that I was shutting myself off from fully experiencing and realizing the enormity of the situation. The more I ignored this nagging the more it continued to grow, to pull harder on my shirtsleeves until I realized that I had to do something with it. And more than just journaling, writing has always been a deeply prayerful activity for me.

I don't know if that nagging was my psyche, begging to try and make sense of all that was happening, or if it was the less-than-subtle invitation of the Holy Spirit to prayer and communion. Likely all of the above. But what I did know was that "if we do not transform our pain, we will most assuredly transmit it."[2] The choice was clear: I have to transform the pain, to allow the presence of God—if it exists at all—to permeate my doubts and questions and heartache; to make something good and beautiful out of something devastating. I had to delve into my religious beliefs and convictions and interrogate them. I had to make it make sense. Make meaning. And I had to let it be used, hopefully, as a balm for somebody else—for fellow strugglers, for those who have lost hope, for those grieving, for parents in situations like ours, to know that you are not alone. As I told my wife Mikhaela, writing this felt like a burden. I don't mean that with negative connotations as much as to say it felt like a weight that needed to be carried until I could unshoulder it.

---

1. Rohr, "Scandal of the Particular."
2. Rohr, "Transforming Pain."

Introduction

As Damayanthi Niles writes, "Theology out of context is vacuous,"³ and as Grace Ji-Sun Kim often says, "Biography is theology."⁴ I hope this writing bears that to be true, because for me to wrestle with these things is to wrestle with life as it has unfolded.⁵ It is extracting theology from biography. Even today it continues to feel pressing, urgent, like an existential demand that I still can't tell whether it's coming from within or without. At this point I'm convinced that trying to differentiate the two would be missing the point anyway. After all, there is no real separation between life and faith. All of life is sacred. And that which is sacred is not different, far off, the ethereal. There is no real distinction between sacred and secular. So when a diagnosis like cancer comes and flips upside-down entire lives, plans, psyches, perspectives on life, and values and priorities, then it means faith is also—and only naturally—put on trial. It must be called to question.

That's how I've needed to process.

Where is "good news" in this? If God is good, why do these things happen? If God is everywhere, where is God in this experience? Can God be trusted?

These aren't lofty or far-off questions. These aren't things to speculate and pontificate about from a safe distance. If Christianity has any merit, it has to mean something to real, lived experiences. Yours and mine. From an oncology ward, these questions are born from a psychological need that is almost palpable. A God who can't be found in suffering can't be found anywhere. Or, at least, isn't worth finding.

The more I live and the more we journey through cancer and the hope for a cure, the more convinced I am that the old Greek

---

3. Niles, *Doing Theology*, 17.

4. Enns, "Episode 29: Grace Ji-Sun Kim," November 13, 2023, in *Faith for Normal People Podcast*, MP3 audio, 11:47–12:00, https://thebiblefornormalpeople.com/episode-29-grace-ji-sun-kim-a-theology-of-visibility/.

5. Randy S. Woodley emphasizes throughout his book *Indigenous Theology and the Western Worldview: A Decolonized Approach to Christian Doctrine* (2022) that story—even personal narrative—is a more biblical and faithful and promising starting point for theology than abstract doctrinal statements or concepts.

Introduction

philosophical notion of God as "the unmoved mover" is unfitting of the God revealed in Christ Jesus. It might be so rooted in the tradition particularly through the dominant European strands of Christianity's insistence on Greek philosophy above all others, but we take our cues from Jesus, not Aristotle or Plato. We look to Jesus for what it means to be human, how to move in the world, and what God is like.[6] We need not understand Jesus through a Platonic lens. As James Cone so clearly articulated, "Christianity begins and ends with the man Jesus—his life, death, and resurrection. He is the Revelation, the special disclosure of God to man, revealing who God is and what his purpose for man is."[7]

What we see in the incarnation—and thus through incarnational eyes—is that God is the *most* moved. There is not even a sparrow that falls from the sky without God knowing.[8] God in Christ suffers alongside, in, and for the healing of the entirety of creation.[9] God cannot be a distant unmoved, unaffected Being. At least, not if we believe God to be perfectly revealed in Jesus.

I hope to somehow address these larger questions of God and suffering, albeit indirectly. Again, I don't attempt to pontificate on theodicy. I don't know why suffering happens. All I know is that it does and that God must be in it, which I mean as both a theological preposition and as an existential plea: God must be in it.

I know that, if at all possible, I have to find C. S. Lewis' words to be true: "I know now, Lord, why you utter no answer. You are yourself the answer. Before your face questions die away. What other answer would suffice?"[10]

My hope in this project is to excavate good news for myself and others on similar journeys by reflecting on our experiences through a pastoral and theological lens with aspects of Christian doctrine as a framework for doing so. To use an analogy, the

---

6. 1 Cor 3:4–11.
7. Cone, *Black Theology*, 34.
8. Matt 10:29–31.
9. The biblical word for salvation—*sozo* or σοζω in the Greek—also implies healing. More on this in the soteriology chapter.
10. Lewis, *Till We Have Faces*, 351.

Introduction

aspects of Christian doctrine are like the lenses of glasses that hopefully make sharper and more apparent beauty, hope, and goodness where we might not have seen any before.

Just as well, I know I'll never be able to do more than simply respond to such weighty questions. I'll never be able to give *the* answer. Because that's not how it works. God, how often I wish it was! But the truth is that what is a satisfying enough answer for me might not be at all for you. And that's OK. God is bigger and more gracious still. God is present wherever we find ourselves, even in the abyss, even in our lack of knowledge, even in our frailty, even in our best attempts at putting things to words, even in the hell that is cancer.[11]

So, to be clear, my hope is not to convince anyone of anything. When pediatric cancer is the threat, arguments mean nothing. Arguments are never really as convincing as we think they are anyway. For me, I sought theology and reasoning as places of comfort but they can only offer so much. They can only penetrate the head and heart so deeply. Often what we want is a formula or reason or logic but what we need are experiences. More specifically, we need experiences of God. We need the Divine to cut through and make God's presence known. We need writing on walls; we need remission and cures; we need a good night's rest; we need fevers to break and no monitor alarms; we need balanced fluid intake and output; we need a good meal; we need our favorite nurses; we need a peace that surpasses understanding.[12] These, too, are the work of God. In this book are some of my own experiences of God's breaking through. Some of which I was fortunate enough to see in the moment and some others only in reflection.

On the oncology floor we need to know that we aren't alone. We need to know that God is here too, even in this. We need to know that God cares enough to hear us and, even more, cares enough to draw nearer still. We need to know that we too can draw nearer to God. We need to know that God is safe. We need to know that God's loving presence is entirely without any hidden threat or

11. See Ps 139:7–10.
12. Phil 4:7.

Introduction

veiled critique or requirement or without any special password or prayer or baptism rite.[13] We need to know that God isn't in need of some hidden faith or prayer quotient before doing something, like some apathetic bureaucrat or narcissistic tyrant who will only heal cancer if he gets enough groveling. We need to know that the poor in spirit[14] really are blessed because, Christ Almighty, we are that in spades. Surely Jesus began his list of Beatitudes with that particular "blessed" for a reason.

God knows we didn't ask for this. We would rather live boring lives, uneventful lives. For these things we pray. We would relish the ability to be mediocre in spirit, to be middle-class in spirit, to be "C's-get-degrees" in spirit, but we are laid low and don't always know if things like trust and hope are actually worth it. How often they seem to let us down, time and again. And we need to know that we can question that, because, oh Lord, do we question it!

If I'm going to be completely honest—and maybe I'm driving the point too much—the responses to such questions like whether God is good and why these bad things happen might be OK today but might not even be satisfying for me next Tuesday. Such is life on this side of the diagnosis. Nothing ever really feels settled. For me, life stopped feeling settled, secure, and predictable on February 16, 2022—the day our son was first diagnosed with leukemia. As I began to write this he's just over a month into a bone marrow transplant which only solidifies how up in the air all of it feels—how day to day absolutely everything is uncertain and unsettled: faith, life, moods, hope, prognosis, the future, the present, even the past. While this is my experience, I'm sure these uncertainties and unsettled feelings are true of all sorts of great sufferings.

And I have to believe that there is grace and mercy and Divine Presence even in this unsettled feeling. In so many ways I think the questions are the point. How do we know that God is good—I mean, really and truly good—unless we can experience that God is good even in the most terrifying and tragic times of

---

13. See Jesus' crucifixion in Luke 23. Interestingly, he never requires baptism or Eucharist or any other sacrament for salvation.

14. Matt 5:1–12.

Introduction

our lives? How can we know that God is ever present and ever caring unless we learn it when we are the most lonely and depressed, swimming in despair? It must be that God also knows this pain as one who suffers with. We must be brave enough to ask the same question that the Son of God cried: "My God, my God, why have you forsaken me?"[15] I had always been confused at what to make of Christ's words on the cross until I lived in an oncology ward with Simon.

By no means do I mean to, even for a moment, imply that God causes cancer. That would not be a good or loving God at all, and I'd run from any theology or person who tried to tell me otherwise. What I do mean to insist is that grace and divine presence abound all the more in suffering, not as a cause but as the abiding presence of the One who brings resurrection and new creation.

And, so, I'm writing this because I need *life*: a fuller life—the kind of life Jesus promises—and for that reason I have to explore and wrestle with my experiences. I have to be honest with myself and God. Hopefully and prayerfully by writing this I can experience again and also infuse into my words the beauty of the Christian faith that I've encountered before if it bears any truth. Perhaps I can be moved by a sense of awe and transcendence. But if I am ever to come face to face with the Way, the Truth, and the Life it will be in an oncology ward. Because this is my life, and now—even after the initial diagnosis—there is no other life available. The track for my life has been set and there is no getting off of it. There are better days and there are anxious, fearful days. May all of them be graced with God's presence, peace, and comfort.

---

15. Matt 27:46.

Mariology

"Because Mary loved [Jesus] more than anyone else did, her pain surpassed the pain of all the others. The higher, the more intense, the sweeter the love, the deeper the sorrow the lover feels when she sees her beloved in pain. Based on my own experience, I am certain that all Christ's disciples and true lovers suffered more harrowing pain than their own dying could ever have caused."[1]

I'VE BEEN A LIFELONG Protestant. More particularly, I grew up swimming in the sea of US evangelicalism in the nineties and early 2000s. Evangelical thought was hard to avoid—not that I tried to at that point in my life—since it has been the loudest and most dominant voice on the American religious scene for decades. Mix that with the tradition I inherited by proxy from my extended family, which is predominantly Pentecostal, and a kid can't help but emphasize certain perspectives on faith while missing out on others. Especially with those two being the prevailing voices I heard. They aren't exactly known to be ecumenical, or to have anything much to say about Mary other than a stale, surface-level recognition that she was Jesus' mom. It was almost like everyone was afraid to talk about Mary too much—let alone with any sort of

---

1. Starr, *Julian of Norwich*, 45.

reverence—because it was "too Catholic." Mary, Jesus' mother, was usually an afterthought or a footnote at best.

All traditions have their strengths and weaknesses, as well as their overemphasized and their underemphasized parts, and I missed out on Mary the *Theotokos*, or "God-bearer," as the Councils of Ephesus (AD 431) and Chalcedon (AD 451) declared and reaffirmed to be a central orthodox doctrine. So who am I to write about Mary?

Certainly I'm not the best person. Mary was, to me, a blip in the story of Jesus for most of my life, if even just a biological necessity. As I see it now, though, if God thought her a good person to raise the Christ, I should probably lean in and learn something from her. You could say I've gotten to know Mary over the last handful of years, and she has since become an invaluable friend in this journey of life. The year before we had Simon, our firstborn, we suffered two miscarriages. It was in that period of loss and grief that Mary first became increasingly important to me. It was because, if for no other reason, she understands suffering and loss. She knows intimately well what it is to lose your beloved child. In her story I find myself reflected back to me.

What first drew me to Mother Mary was that she, like I, was not the one who faced her own death. She had to come face-to-face with the threat against the life of her beloved child. In the miscarriages, and in Simon's cancer journey, I was a spectator. It was not my body that bled like Mikhaela's or Simon's or Christ's. I, like Mary, was standing, witnessing, and mourning, powerless to stop anything. And, yet, being a witness is holy work, too.

Even after that sorrowful introduction to the mother of Jesus, I'd like to think we have more in common than just traumatic experiences. None of us ought to be reduced down to our greatest hurts. We all hold magnitudes of life and love and stories within us, if even at times they might all be seen through that very particular lens of sorrow.

Believing there to be more to our connection than hurt, I find myself thinking of her often, reflecting on her life, her Magnificat, the theological and ethical and social depth of her proclamations,

Mariology

what it must have been like to be Jesus' mother, and how she might have given form and shape to Jesus in his earliest years. I see now Mary is not just some woman. She is the mother of Christ. Mary, the mother of God. Mary, the one who taught wisdom himself. Her particulars are significant. And, at times, all too relatable.

While it may be strange for a guy with my background to start a book by talking about Mary, to talk about Mary is to talk about being a parent to a child whom you love and treasure. It is to stand a witness to their strength and to their suffering. With these things I can relate. Many of us can.

Mary, mother of the crucified one, friend and mother of us all, pray for us. Pray for us who can't do anything but bear witness. Pray for us who have to muster the bravery of facing the day. Pray for us who all we have to offer is our meager presence.

To Be Known

"To know your own body is a spiritual care and protection. To know the body of another is a spiritual union and conciliation."[2]

We were very fortunate with Simon's medical team for the most part. Medically, I'm sure they are all superb, but there is more to medicine than addressing diseases and ailments and afflictions. There is heart. There is psyche. There is soul. The whole person must be tended to, must be nurtured.

We were doubly fortunate to both be able to spend all of our days with him in the hospital. My church told me to not even worry about anything to do with my job, and that our youth group—a primary responsibility of mine—would be run as long as it needed to be by our youth group leaders. Mikhaela was able to take medical leave, and, being a teacher, her school district even called an emergency board meeting to approve of her leave. The teachers she works with, and the ones at other schools in the district, donated

---

2. Riley, *This Here Flesh*, 66.

their own sick days to her to cover the rest of the school year so that Mikhaela could keep her paycheck and our health insurance.

With both of us staying at the hospital with our newborn baby, and with Simon being so young—just four-and-a-half months old when first diagnosed—he really needed us there. We needed each other there, too. Life can be cruel and harsh. We need not live it alone.

The day the world stood still we spent most of it in the emergency room holding our lethargic, septic, and leukemia-ridden baby. His lung partially collapsed, his breathing a rhythmic grunting for air. The doctors could do all that they could do, but what could we do? To sit down felt like an insult. To stand felt too towering, too strong, too sure-footed.

Mikhaela held Simon in her arms doing what she does best: she was loving our baby. I don't think she thought about it. She just did it. Through her tears she cooed and gently rocked. She shushed and ran her fingertips over his skin. We weren't feeling what he was feeling, but we could make sure he knew he wasn't alone. Mom and Dad were always right next to him.

In times like these—times where you don't know what to do, how to do it, or even what is good and helpful—thank God for people who do. Joe was the emergency room nurse that day. He was swift and careful, personal and informative. He told us the best thing we could do was eat, so he ordered us chicken tenders and fries. We hadn't eaten all day. We didn't feel like eating, but we did anyway. Sometimes it's a grace to have someone tell you what to do, to reveal to you what you need but are unable to see in yourself.

At one point while Mikhaela was holding Simon she said the fear out loud: *I don't know how to help him.* Joe, moving at the pace and urgency of an emergency room nurse, stopped what he was doing. He knelt beside the hospital bed to look Mikhaela in her eyes. "You're doing great, Mom. You are doing exactly what he needs."

This became a theme that I now see has been present throughout all of Simon's treatments: to know and to be known.

Mariology

We heard it from doctors and nurses all throughout the hospital. *Nobody knows your baby like you do.* It was often said in a clinical way. Employed as a way of asking what his baseline behavior was, or if he was in pain from the surgery, or how he was handling the chemotherapy. But, to be honest, we were just getting to know our baby. Likely, he had leukemia since birth. As a baby he was tired all of the time, barely able to stay awake an hour and a half before needing a nap. On top of that, he was our firstborn. We didn't know—not really—what babies were like. We didn't know *him*. We got to know him and his little personality after he started chemotherapy. Imagine that—he felt better after he started chemotherapy. Poor little guy, he must have felt awful all the time.

But sometimes it would be said in a much more tender way. A way in which the words carry a holy resonance, a recognition of the sacred relationship between parent and child. It was a way of inviting us into his healing. We were part of the team. We weren't just parents who had to stay sidelined. We could give him what nobody else could. We could give him his Mom and Dad. We could supply endless love, boundless patience, limitless affection, and unceasing adoration. To love is holy work.

We took it to heart. Nobody did know our baby like we did. Even if we, in our own way, were also just getting to know him. Even still, nobody else spent as much time with him as we did. They couldn't have even if they wanted to.

We became his fiercest advocates. We pushed back against nurses and doctors when necessary. We pressed issues. We demanded answers and time to take our questions. We were the ones who caught that his body became addicted to morphine in the bone marrow unit before the doctors would really entertain the idea. When he would have surgeries and procedures they would ask us how he does with sedation, and we would tell them that he's a bear to sedate. Usually they would brush this off but would always say something afterwards: "You were right. We had to give him more than usual before he would go out."

Not that anyone was openly hostile or acted as if they didn't have time for us. This all takes a more combative tone than was usually given. But our pushbacks and insistence were the sign of something inside of us as his parents. It was a growing internal confidence. He was our first and we hadn't even been parents for half of a year yet, but, still, we grew into ourselves.

But this coming into ourselves doesn't happen in isolation. Some understandings of theology tell us that Jesus' divine personhood found its culmination in Gethsemane. But we don't need scholars to know that his foundations were laid long before. Most notably by his mother.

I think something magical happens when we step into this kind of deep and intimate knowing of someone else. Something alchemical. It is a knowledge of other and a knowledge of self. They grow hand in hand. I know myself because I know another. To me this is what it means to be a parent. Just like it is what it means to be married. Put simply in other words, it's the gift of love. Not that my identity is eclipsed or totally contingent on my being a parent, but that my self-understanding is deepened and enriched in being one. It is made more vibrant and clearer. It is a crucible and testing ground as much as it is an invitation to a truer part of yourself. It is a deepening and enlivening. I think I was made for this. But, to be honest, I think we all were made to know and be known. We were all designed to love and be loved. There is no better theology or ethic than love.

I wonder if Mary ever felt the same way—that she knew a little more about herself because of the blessing of her son. I think she must have. How else could she sing a song like this: "My soul glorifies the Lord and my spirit rejoices in God my Savior, for he has been mindful of the humble state of his servant. From now on all generations will call me blessed, for the Mighty one has done great things for me—holy is his name."[3] We see the reciprocal nature of love in her words. That deepening of self and understanding. Transfigured by what she gives and what has been given to her. She knew what a blessing she is, because of the blessing she has been given, and the blessing that she is to her beloved. It is a near Trinitarian formula. And it is grace and mystery.

3. Luke 1:46–49.

Nobody knows your baby like you. Teach us, O *Theotokos*, the contours of God's face. What did you learn about God, by feeding him at your breast? How did he like to be rocked? Slowly swaying in your arms or with short bounces? What was revealed to you in those tender early morning hours? What was the Word's first word? What was his favorite color? What games did he love so much? Did he like being thrown up into the air? Or would he clutch your wrists with that look—that *don't let me go* look? Teach us, *Theotokos*, the contours of God's face.

Christ's Teacher

The Scriptures say that Jesus "grew in wisdom and stature, and in favor with God and humanity."[4] The savior of the world had to learn the depths of what salvation means. The healer of the cosmos had to learn the wisdom of healing and its relationship to suffering. The image had to grow up. It's a beautiful reminder of Jesus' humanity. From whom do we imagine he learned these things but from his mother?

Wisdom is not just imparted. Like yeast in dough it has to be worked through the whole body.[5] It is gained from our experiences. There was a conversation we had with Simon's primary oncologist, Dr. Saini, that moved us both so much that we went away floored by her words and wisdom. As we talked about it, the words just flowed out from me: "That's hard-won wisdom." There are some truths that we can't know without experience.

Even still, wisdom is not just learned from our own experiences—be it from a classroom, an oncology floor, in sacred Scripture, in a recovery group, or in a church. Wisdom is also passed down. It is in the nurture and prayers of mothers late at night. It is in fathers who instill gentleness, love, and kindness by embodying these virtues.

---

4. Luke 2:52.
5. See Matt 13:33.

Bone of My Bone

Our parents and guardians—those earliest nurturers—are our first teachers. We learn emotions from them, boundaries, rights and wrongs, how to eat, how to sit up, how to share, how to play, how to dream, even what to dream and hope for. One time Simon was role-playing as me and speaking to an imaginary Simon in the room. Evidently imaginary Simon did something he shouldn't have because Simon-turned-me said, "Dude. Why did you do that?" I had no idea I say that at all, let alone enough for it to be a regular phrase of mine, but, when I heard him say it, I could hear myself say it. Like we've already said, parenting is an exercise in knowing and being known. And, more than that, this playful moment was a sobering alert. Simon is learning from me how to parent some day, how to respond to accidents and bad choices, how to react when someone does wrong. Lord, have mercy.

Mary is that first teacher for Jesus. When we look at the life of Jesus, and consider that he had to grow in wisdom and stature, how much of his wisdom was first planted in him by his mother? Mary, the wise teacher for the Christ, the Son of God. What a beautiful and human thing. He had to learn and grow "in wisdom," and God, in God's infinite wisdom, trusted a young Mary with the task.

What all did Jesus learn from his mother? Would it be overstepping to say that she laid the foundation for everything? I don't think so. It's true for each one of us. It must surely be true for Jesus as well. How many words or phrases did he say, even into his adulthood, that he had said all his life, and learned as a toddler from Mary? Maybe he used so many metaphors about agriculture and plants and animals because his mom was an avid gardener or enjoyed a slow walk outside. Maybe Mary would let herself be raptured by beauty. Maybe Jesus picked up on this habit: "consider the lilies."[6]

Unfortunately, we don't get many of Mary's teachings in Scripture, but we do have a beautiful song: The Magnificat. The Magnificat isn't just some scriptural passage as if it could be detached from a real person who lived a real life in a real context with real implications. Hers is an incendiary religious, social, and

---

6. Luke 12:27 NRSVue.

political poem. It informed and influenced her son, the Messiah. And it is countercultural and radically subversive and hopeful.

He must have learned of God's preferential option for the poor, the marginalized, and the dispossessed from his mom in addition to the biblical stories he grew up on.[7] Like Broderick Greer wrote, "When we listen to Mary's son, we get a sense that her rebel anthem moonlighted as Jesus' lullaby."[8]

Who is this one who taught the Christ how to live and move and have his being?[9]

The Treasure of the Heart: A Description

"But Mary treasured up all these things and pondered them in her heart."[10]

My appreciation and reverence for Mary sprouted in our first two pregnancies and grew fruit when Mikhaela was pregnant with Simon. As with most good things it didn't happen all at once. Mikhaela was well into her pregnancy and it was around the time that I started to be able to see little movements through her belly—feel little feet and fists press outward—that Mary started to be a source of reflection for me. Particularly significant to me has been the verse about Mary treasuring everything to do with her newborn baby. That verse grew roots that have spread and made a home in the soil of my soul and hasn't left since. It made such a lasting impression because, if I may be so bold, I felt a bit like Mary did.

It is a treasure—a thing more precious than anything that could be bought, or crafted, or found, or discovered. It is a pure gift to become a parent. The feeling of joy and ecstasy of burgeoning parenthood still resides deep within, a bliss frozen in time in the

---

7. See Luke 1:46–55.
8. Greer, "Mary's Rebel Anthem."
9. See Acts 17:28.
10. Luke 2:19.

cells of my body. A well I continue to visit and drink from. It is a somatic memory. I can conjure up those same feelings.

Perhaps that is both a testament to the power of joy and to the power of joy on the other side of nearly losing your treasured baby. The joy of parenthood is always accessible, just now textured with all that comes with raising growing children. Not every day is easy, but most frustrations and hardships are tinged with gratitude. I'm glad both of my boys are still here with me. I am thankful that I have my firstborn to be able to be annoyed with. I treasure that gift.

I don't believe that kind of accessible joy is limited to people who have faced life or death scenarios. It just takes intentionality. As it does for all of us. Because it is a joy that is deeply personal, yet wildly, furiously, and terrifyingly beyond one's own self. It is personal and particular, but transcendent. Finite and infinite. It is a joy that connects me to parents throughout time and space. Of my own, it is mine, yet not unique.

There is a picture from the moment Simon was born that our dear friend Brittany took, who is a labor and delivery nurse, and it captures my experience beautifully. My jaw absolutely slack, lower than I knew possible, a smile beaming across my face, and eyes wider than they ever have been before. Bewildered at the beauty of my firstborn, overwhelmed with joy, and stunned at Mikhaela's strength and grace.

No amount of classes or listening to other people's experiences could have prepared me for the moments when our babies were born. Everyone always tells you how hard parenting is and how there are so many things that you can't know until you're in it. As if they are saying, "It's hard. Harder than you can even imagine." But after the two losses, I was glad to get up early with the baby so Mikhaela could sleep. I was happy to have my REM cycles interrupted in order to comfort, rock, and burp my babies before setting them back in their bassinet. I don't miss the sleep. I know that in ten years' time, I won't think back and say, "Man, I just really wish I got more sleep when my kids were babies." I know that what I will feel is gratitude for those late nights and early morning snuggles. I will understand more fully that they were invitations to abide in love.

Even still, God willing, there will be a day when Simon and Jack will grow and not need me in that same way anymore. I might as well treasure the stages they are in now. Because both phases of life are grace: the missed sleep now and the day when they don't need me in the same way. I don't want to miss the baby phase while I have it. And I will do my best to welcome and celebrate and find joy in the next phases as they come too.

I don't think anyone ever really spent as much time talking to me about how absolutely beautiful parenting is. If they did, I didn't have ears to hear it. In my memory, everyone just tried to prepare me for the loss of sleep. Nobody mentioned how spectacular it is to have diapers that I need to change. Or how wonderful it is that all of my clothes don't really matter anymore, because they are no longer just mine. They have become giant burp rags and booger wipes. Nobody prepared me for how prayerful and spiritual it is to stare at a newborn's uncoordinated movements and watch as their blinking eyes soak in and trace the outline of your face. I've heard they do this because their little brains are unable to input so much detail. Maybe that's what John meant when he said no one has ever seen the face of God.[11] Maybe we're all just newborns who can only stand to trace the outline of God's face. It would be too much to look at God straight on, so we steal glimpses and glances and peripheries. Perhaps we see "only a reflection as in a mirror"[12] out of necessity.

No one ever explained how I would look at this newborn baby in the eyes—the baby who has only been in the world for a handful of days—and begin to understand so much more about God, about life, and about love. There's a reason Jesus' words still shock us when we take them seriously: that God is not some far-off monarch or uncaring demiurge that we have to approach with a mixture of the right words, contrition, and honorifics. God relates to us, as Jesus taught, as a Father, a parent. This is not hopeful

---

11. See John 1:18 and 1 John 4:12.
12. See 1 Cor 13:12.

idealism on our part. It is God's disclosure; God's revelation. Jesus teaches us that God is our parent, because God first sees us as God's beloved children.

Could it be that God's heart swells and bursts over and over again each time he looks into our eyes?

In a flash, as I sat on the couch and stared at my newborn baby held in my arms, my beliefs and understandings shifted on so much. So much became so much clearer. All the things that plague humanity, that demean and harm—things like violence, racism, incarceration, the death penalty, LGBTQ+ discrimination, hunger, poverty, homelessness, and hell—all got drastically reevaluated because of my love for this little baby. As many true conversions, it was both in an instant and a process. And it began out of the love for and beauty of my baby. This little baby who is mine and who I just met.

I realized that I can't imagine any good, loving God to be cruel and vindictive and judgmental and angry, or even uncaring, uncommitted, unmoved, and uninvolved.[13] I can't imagine that a God who is love would have to be beholden to any of our modern American understandings. I have to imagine that God is a better Father than I can be, or could ever imagine being. "If you, then, though you are evil, know how to give good gifts to your children, how much more will your Father in heaven give good gifts to those who ask him!"[14] As much as I love my children, and have been moved and softened and deepened by them, how much more powerful and transformative must God's love for all of God's children be. How much more God must be affected by His looking into the eyes of His beloved.

Love alone is good theology. Or, as Hans Urs von Balthasar said with unmixed words in his momentous book *Love Alone Is Credible*, "Lovers are the ones who know most about God; the

---

13. If God is love, as 1 John 4:8 says, then Paul's descriptors of love in 1 Cor 13 are descriptors of the nature of God. Read 1 Cor 13 and replace the word "love" with the word "God" and meditate on it for a good, long while. Does that look like the God you know?

14. Matt 7:11.

theologian must listen to them."[15] By grace, in the process of becoming a parent, I grew into a lover. Not just a theorist or a thinker but a person who has been plunged into the deeper reality that undergirds the cosmos: love. In that conversion-by-love, I left behind my secret "what-if" holdovers of believing in a possibly-or-at-least-otherwise-vengeful deity from evangelicalism and found myself embodying a deeper truth: God is love. God, for me, is best found in this experience of fatherhood, of interrupted nights, of changing diapers, of staring into wild and skittish eyes. And we are the treasure in the heart of the divine.

The Treasure of the Heart: Living wisdom

You can imagine that when our baby boy—our firstborn after two devastating losses—was diagnosed with leukemia it felt like our world was crumbling. It was theologically, emotionally, psychologically, and existentially crushing. It felt like the goodness of God's creation was coming apart at the seams. Our best-laid plans dashed against the rocks of life's storms. The joy and honor of my life was threatened in an instant with oblivion.

What do you do on the worst day of your life?

I think Mary's wisdom—to treasure and to ponder in her heart—is not just a descriptor, but is an invitation for all of life, and, certainly not least of all, in moments of fear and despair. It is as much a parental description as it is an intentional act of reverence. It is the holy practice of a deep abiding presence to the moment.

To say it another way, what we see in Mary is praxis. It is an invitation to do as she did. It is the invitation to cherish the moment, to be where your feet are, to stay present to the information that is right in front of you, and to revere the good, the true, and the beautiful whenever and wherever you can. All of which can feel impossible when your child's life is on the line. It is to deliberately celebrate the small victories, and to cherish each moment. To not

---

15. Balthasar, *Love Alone Is Credible*, 8.

be swept away in the "what-ifs." It is the invitation to treasure all the beauty that is around you, even amidst the swirling chaos, and to spend time pondering all the goodness in your innermost being. It is a sacred practice done often in existential rebellion against the crushing reality that looms overhead.

All of which have been soul-saving for me through the journey of my son's cancer. As anyone who has experienced a diagnosis like cancer knows, the "what-ifs" are legion. As Dr. Saini, Simon's primary oncologist, impressed on us in the ICU when he was first diagnosed, it is crucial to practice "reigning in the mind." Mary's wisdom to treasure and ponder is the re-grounding practice when the ground is taken away.

Which is exactly what a cancer diagnosis feels like. It feels like the bottom of everything falls away and you find yourself in a vacuous abyss. You have become eclipsed. Isolated and alone. Within an abyssal prison all your own. Where is God in this? Where could God possibly be?

I don't know your story or your experiences but I'm sure your life has been marked by loss and grief, sorrow and heartache. So it is to be human; so it is to be alive. We all face loss and heartache. Suffering is unavoidable. It feels so much like a derailing of life. Like being irrevocably put on a path that you shouldn't be on. It feels like an agonizing homesickness. Suffering tunes our hearts towards a long-forgotten Edenic existence that must be somewhere in our souls; longing for a time of the restoration of all things. We long for things to be made right, to be made whole, to be made new. But suffering is just part of it. To exist is to belong to the universal community of co-sufferers. There is no going around it.

Following Mary's wisdom to treasure and to ponder amidst suffering is a hopefully defiant act in the face of hopelessness. It is to kick and scream against the looming abyss and the despair within it. It is to proclaim that light and hope persist; that love and healing transcend even death.

Even as I was writing this book, I went back and wanted to be able to describe the abyss. To give it language, and by doing so, somehow give it shape and definition. Which, said another way, means to give it limits, to give it boundaries. As if that were possible. As if I should.

But you know the abyss. You are intimately familiar with the groundlessness. I can't describe it any more than you already know it. Yet, what I hope to humbly offer is that God is the abyss. The theological term is "apophatic theology." It is theology of negation, of wordlessness. I imagine, especially if your suffering was a while ago, you already know this to be true, too. It is a paradox. The abyss is filled. In the groundlessness is the ground of being. In the void is the presence of God.

A God Like Mary

While Mary's wisdom is a grounding—and re-membering[16]—practice for us, it serves, too, as a description of God as parent. In our own act of treasuring and pondering comes the sublime realization that that same kind of unrelenting love and treasuring is always directed towards us, too.

God's own love meets us in the act of treasuring. As we treasure, we get a glimpse of how much we are treasured. This is the pondering that accompanies the treasuring—when we ponder in our hearts our own beloved, we realize how treasured we are by God. How much God treasures me too, even as I hurt, even in my confusion and doubts and sorrow and fear; even as I hurl insults from my pain-induced agnosticism. God, like Mary did with her baby, treasures and ponders all the little things about us in God's own heart. Like I have done with my babies. Perhaps, too, like you have done with your own.

This divine love, in which I am always the subject, being true for me means it is also true for everyone. And to ponder God's beloved-ness towards other people is an invitation to step into that flow of love—to participate in loving them. To put it

---

16. Meaning that to treasure and ponder puts us back together. It is the apophatic theology of the abyss: in the face of groundlessness I push against it and its accompanying despair to choose to live into the love and beauty that is here now, empowered by the presence of God that fills even the void.

phenomenologically, when I gaze in love at my children I wake up to the reality that I, too, am held in the gaze of God's love. When I ponder that reality, I realize that God's love as Father isn't just for me but for everyone in the same way. Which, in turn, expands the scope of my own love. It grows from a nearsighted love into a more expansive love. My perspective and my love grows to include the nurses, doctors, music therapists, custodians, cafeteria workers, physical therapists, occupational therapists, social workers.

Which is exactly the balm we need in the midst of hellish experiences. We need a deep resonance to know that we are not alone. Experiences like these are already so isolating—physically, emotionally, socially, psychologically, even spiritually. We need the force of love to break open our myopic perspective to realize the web of love all around. A web that we are entangled in and invited to participate in. We are nestled into a web of solidarity with all other people as co-sufferers, but we are also all, at the same time and in the same place, held together by the very stuff of God: love.

And we have Mary to thank, who gives us that sense of radiant warmth to round this understanding out. Jesus, undoubtedly shaped by his mom's deep love for him, intentionally draws our understanding to see God as *our* heavenly parent. What is true of Mary towards Jesus is tenfold of God towards all people. God treasures and ponders us. Just as we treasure and ponder the miracle of children.[17]

A Compassionate God

Believing God treasures and ponders each person becomes all that much more confusing when tragedy strikes, the diagnosis is cancer, there is a sudden loss or natural disaster, and entire lives are

---

17. Though this is my own experience, which has very much been shaped by being a dad, I know many aunties and uncles—biological and chosen family—who also treasure and ponder children. By no means does biology mean Mary's wisdom will be followed, nor does it mean you have to have children in order to treasure and ponder. Jesus had no children but surely treasured and pondered (see Matt 19:14).

upended. It brings into question God's love, character, and ability. Even God's existence is a live question for debate. A diagnosis like cancer becomes an arrow that pierces into the deepest part of us, the softest and most tender part of ourselves, where we are most vulnerable and slowest to heal. And there is no sharper threat than one aimed at our children. There are some wounds that will never fully heal, not really—be they physical, emotional, or psychological. Thank God for therapists and loving community.

There are no easy answers for any of this. It's a journey of discovery and rediscovery and of hard-won wisdom that nobody would choose. Yet, what we choose to do within our circumstances and these lives that we wish were otherwise makes all the difference. This experience, too, can be a teacher. Cancer, even, can teach us about Christ. It can give us enough reflection and contemplation for multiple lifetimes. It is in the experience of my son's diagnosis, treatment, relapse, and bone marrow transplant that I not only understood but experienced that the co-suffering love of God in Christ Jesus is central to everything. The entire cosmos is cruciform.[18] In God there is solidarity with all suffering. As Paul wrote, speaking of Jesus, "Who, being in very nature God, did not consider equality with God something to be used to his own advantage; rather, he made himself nothing by taking the very nature of a servant, being made in human likeness. And being found in appearance as a man, he humbled himself by becoming obedient to death—even death on a cross!"[19] The solidarity of God is such. It is solidarity in all of our circumstances and experiences even to death.

In God there is a deep empathy. It is shared experience. Human experience is assumed into the divine life. So much so that God is full of compassion, which etymologically means that God "suffers with." So much so that the crucifixion, aside from the beginning of the triumph of sin, death, and hell, is also God's eternal solidarity with all sufferers. Be they people watching as Alzheimer's

18. Delio, *Emergent Christ*, 119. See also Irenaeus, *On the Apostolic Preaching*, 62.

19. Phil 2:6–8.

ravages their loved one's mind or polar bears drowning because of global warming and melting ice caps. Solidarity in suffering with all creation is the nature of divine Trinitarian love.[20] As Dan Migliore wrote, "Only a suffering God can help us, but the suffering God is the triune God whose holy, self-giving, victorious love is at work from the creation of the world to its completion."[21]

Only a suffering God can help us.

Or, as Ilia Delio writes:

> The self-gift of the Father to the Son reflects a self-emptying already within the heart of God in such a way that we may think of the cross first in the heart of God before it is in the heart of creation. The very act of creation reflects something of a "divine crucifixion," for in creation God reveals the divine power to be God's own unconditional love for the world. The act of descending into what is nothing—creation—in order to express Godself is God's humility, God's condescension, God's going outside the divine riches to become poor. The cross is key not only to sin and human nature, but to God. The cross reveals to us the heart of God because it reveals the vulnerability of God's love.[22]

Why? Why is God so committed to solidarity?

Because God, like Mary with her son, watches you, loves you, and has treasured all these things of your life and pondered them in his heart. If for no other reason, like a parent, to see you suffer is an experience of God's own type of suffering. Like a parent, God's own wellbeing is wrapped up in the wellbeing of his children.

If only we could embody this same depth of compassion with one another. Many people offer sympathy: "I care about your suffering," while even that feels uncomfortable for many. Too often we opt for pity, if anything: "I acknowledge your suffering."[23] As Robert Shelton illustrates in Dr. Neel Burton's article, the move from

---

20. Delio, *Emergent Christ*, 121.
21. Migliore, *Faith Seeking Understanding*, 136.
22. Delio, *Emergent Christ*, 121.
23. Burton, "Difference Between Empathy and Sympathy."

pity to sympathy to empathy to compassion is a sliding scale based off of a person's own engagement in the experience of another. The move towards compassion hinges on personal engagement, not just feelings. It is about personal investment. To say that God is compassionate and is in solidarity with God's beloved children is to say that God is fully invested. God suffers and is vulnerable because God is inextricably invested in the wellbeing of creation—is fully invested in your wellbeing. "Only a suffering God can help us."

Most people, in my experience, are afraid of entering into difficult emotions like grief and choose to stay on the lower side of engagement. This is especially true in other people's grief, but, unfortunately, is not uncommon in their own grief as well. The Christian call, if we are to be the body of Christ, is to lean into the hard work of engagement. It is to meet people in their suffering. If only a suffering God can help us, then only a suffering church can help us, too. Solidarity is one of the most significant things we can do as people.

As a parent of a child with cancer, I can say that the difference in people's level of engagement is palpable. It becomes an incredible balm when someone is willing to empathize, let alone embody the sacredness of true compassion.[24] As tremendously helpful as a GoFundMe is to pay for transportation, bills, food, loss of work, etc., nothing tends to the soul like someone who is willing to sit with you, to listen to you, to ask you deep questions, and to give ample space for uncomfortable answers.

The book of Job is a tremendous example. His friends do so, so well. Then they start talking. They appear to enflesh a beautiful example of compassion, and then they pull back from the discomfort and isolate Job in his grief by offering explanations. Never underestimate the power of a nonjudgmental, agendaless presence.

---

24. I think most people probably assume themselves to be more compassionate than their actions would lead a person suffering to experience. I know this to be true of myself even still. It is easier for me to share some words to skirt having to listen to someone else's pain.

As an aside, I now read Job much differently. I used to imagine God correcting Job, rhetorically laying into him: "Where were you when I laid the earth's foundation? Tell me, if you understand."[25] I thought God's response to be belittling, insensitive. Now I see it as an invitation to mystery. Less that God is saying, "Who are you to question me and my holiness/plan/action/inaction/etc.?," and more that God is saying, "Trust me. I know it hurts. I know you are drowning in pain and grief. Will you trust me today? I, the one who laid the foundations of the world, am also good, loving, and present to you in your suffering. Even hurt and even death is also a grace-filled transition. I know it hurts, but I can care for them in such tender and powerful ways even in death."

But even if that sounds too good to be true, or you find yourself uncomfortable with a God who is compassionate—a God who suffers—or you find yourself wrapped up in a concept of "holiness" that means you can't question God,[26] or you're just not even sure where you're at right now with faith, we can also find empathy and solidarity in Mary. Which can be helpful because God, for many, is a loaded word. Whether it's because of tough relationships with our own parents, church hurts, poor representations of God's character from once-trusted teachers, a healthy amount of skepticism, nebulous and intangible concepts of God, or because of whatever else "God" can be tough to connect with.

In this instance, the very human, very concrete Mary still holds empathy and solidarity with us. We need not it to even be metaphysical. She is a fellow sufferer. What we see in Mary is one who knows this kind of pain that cuts to the core. She knows what it is to see her child, the one whom she loves, suffer. The one whose every action since he was a baby is treasured in her heart. She witnessed him suffer and ultimately die. Mary is intimate with fear and loss, as well as the deepest wisdom that the things we love most should also be held with open hands. In Mary we see a friend, a confidant, a fellow sufferer.

---

25. Job 38:4.

26. When we "question God" we are more accurately questioning our concepts and frameworks of God.

Mariology

Solvitur Ambulando

As I've already mentioned, before our son Simon was born we suffered two miscarriages. What I didn't already mention is that both of these miscarriages happened in the same year, in the height of the COVID-19 lockdown phase in the United States.

By grace, we live in a city that has great bike trails, and, in the winter when the trees are bare, we can see a nature preserve. In fact, to walk from our front door to the preserve's lookout point is exactly half of a mile. A fact learned during that time when there was nothing else to do but walk.

We had started going on walks just about every day during lockdown. It was secluded, private enough, and in the instance we did pass by someone, I would hold my breath, which serves as an illustration of the growing anxiety and fear that would multiply within me over the next four years. I was never much of an anxious person until this time of life.

These walks that we would take, however emotionally turbulent they might have been at times, became a cherished ritual. They are a balm to my anxious soul. These near-daily walks were good for the body, but even better for our hearts and minds. They became a physical way to walk out the anxiety and became a type of praying with our feet. Even before a cancer diagnosis ever came. Even before one of our babies was born. Even in the midst of grief and uncertainty in the wake of miscarriages. We were being met by and grown in a grace that would help us later.

I remember the tangible sensation, each walk did something inside. Each step was inconsequential but the walk as a whole was life-giving. Nourishing. By the time Mikhaela and I would get back home—but usually at some point in the middle of it—we would be standing a little taller, moving a little lighter, feeling more connected to each other and the world around us. Each walk gave a little something that we needed: a type of daily bread.

I remember learning a lot about myself, what I believed, and what I didn't. Wrestling with fears and anxieties and having to learn over and over during each walk that "people are not the problem." Maybe it was just me, maybe it was exaggerated by my personality, maybe it was the loss of the two babies, but during COVID I became cynical and jaded, frustrated at the surges of infection and seeing people still going out and visiting people and having parties, keeping the numbers of cases in our city growing. *Remember, Grant: people are not the problem. A virus is.* I'd have to remind myself of this, even as I held my breath and smiled and waved at the other pilgrims on the bike trail. Grace works in us slowly.

So when we lost our first baby—affectionately called "Peanut"—we did what we had already learned to do: walk. There's a phrase sometimes attributed to Saint Augustine that says, "It is solved by walking." *Solvitur ambulando.*

This was very much our experience. Yet, I would nuance it. I don't think wounded-ness and heartache work the same way. I wouldn't say anything was "solved," but I would say that a whole lot was healed by walking. "Solved" implies a problem that can be overcome and left behind, like math homework or a crossword. "Healing" is more true to the human experience and our wounds. It is an ongoing process. It is continual. It is cyclical. It is a wound that, as it heals, becomes a scar. A scar that, even years later, remains sensitive. Like the one on the tip of my finger from a mandolin slicer. Even years later the skin feels different. It bears the trauma, the nerves more sensitive. Just because the flesh has grown back and the wound has covered over it is not "solved" but it has healed. Perhaps you, too, have your own still-sensitive scars.

Grief is healed, in fits and starts, by connecting to the life that teems all around. By breathing in the joy of beauty. By connections with good friends. Isolation begins to be healed when we recognize the way that all life is interconnected. To be alive is to live a story within a greater story, alongside every other story.

As we walked we healed. Which, of course, means that we grieved. We had to. I'm skeptical of any significant healing that doesn't enter into a grieving process. We mourned. We cried. We expressed our frustrations, our confusions, our hopes, our feelings of being duped by God, of being let down, of being forsaken. But there is another layer of grief: the stories you tell yourself about your own experiences. A second order of reflection. Not just reflecting on the circumstances, but reflecting on what you're thinking and feeling about the circumstances.

We contemplated our grief. We swam into the depths of our hurt. It was a terribly vulnerable experience, but one that was met with the strangest warmth of comfort. A comfort that felt as if it came from outside of us while, at the same time, also came from within us. Sitting in grief is like partaking in the Eucharist: remembering Christ's body broken and his blood spilled. Even in broken bodies, shattered dreams, and lost hope there is Immanuel—there is God with us.

In Christ's own broken body we find God's presence. Why should it not be so with our own?

If God is large enough to be present even in the death of Christ, God is large enough to be just as present in our own hurt, loss, and suffering. It is my deepest and firmest conviction that there is no experience that is alien to God. Perhaps most acutely of all is suffering. This solidified for me after Simon's diagnosis. When you leave life and "normalcy" to live in a hospital, watching your baby fight for his life, faith gets leveled to ground zero. Most things are burned away. The wheat is separated from the chaff. For me the gold that stayed from life's refining fire is the conviction that God is never absent or detached from life—any part of it, especially suffering.

This is, for me, the grounding principle of all pastoral and theological work.

God is not beyond human experience. God in Christ is the most human human. Somehow that brings—or, at least brought for us—a strange kind of comfort. We have all experienced bad attempts at comfort. The kind that dismisses our hurt, usually with pithy comments like "God has a plan" or, even worse, the implication that it was because of our lack of faith, a test of faith, or because we didn't pray enough. Would a God whose plan it is to give a child cancer be worth following?

God in Christ bearing the fullness of human life and experience isn't the kind of comfort that tries to rush healing. This compassionate healing is a long, slow, daily walk. It is airing out all of your complaints and doing it again day after day. It is one that meets us where we are and doesn't try to make us be somewhere we are not.

As Paul alludes, we can know Christ not just in the power of his resurrection but also in suffering.[27] Hopefully it also comes with the hope of resurrection—of new life—on the other side of grief. But sometimes even rushing to hope can feel like a betrayal of the magnitude of our pain.

Only the slow, healing walk with a God who sees, knows, and experiences hurt and grief is healing. *Solvitur ambulando*. We cannot rush to hope for healing. If we don't want to be consumed by the circumstances, we cannot ignore the painful realities. And we must face them daily. All we can do is walk, and, on our walk, trust that the Lord will meet with us—will meet us on our own road to Emmaus.[28]

Love Beyond Hell

As I said earlier, when Simon was born I remember so vividly holding him in my arms, looking at his sweet newborn face, and being washed over with a sudden and embodied feeling and realization that if God is Father, or parent, like Jesus teaches,[29] and if God's very essence is love,[30] then how much more love does God have for me, and him, and everyone? As I looked down at this newborn scrunched in my arms, it hit me that I would do or give anything for him. Immediately with that thought came another: God must feel the same way. God feels that way for me, for him, for you, for

---

27. See Phil 3:10–11.
28. Luke 24:13–35.
29. See the Lord's Prayer in Matt 6:9–13 or Luke 11:2–4 for examples.
30. 1 John 4:8.

Mariology

everybody who ever was, is, or will be. This is the radical teaching of Jesus to talk about God not just as Lord, but as a dear parent.

And just as quickly as those epiphanies came, so did another follow-up thought: that it is ludicrous to believe that God sends people to eternal conscious torment, let alone allow them to "choose it."[31] I would move heaven and earth for my kids, and the entire Christian belief is that God has done exactly that.

Even more, the Christian Scriptures attest that God descended into the realm of the dead[32] to save those who were held captive to the destructive powers of sin, hell, and death.[33] "For the Word unfolded himself everywhere, above and below and in the depths and in the breadth: above, in creation; below, in the incarnation; in the depths, in hell; in breadth, in the world. Everything is filled with the knowledge of God. . . . For in both ways the Savior exercised his love for human beings through his incarnation, in that he both banished death from us and renewed us."[34] How could a God who has already conquered sin, death, and Hades let his beloved be trapped in eternal conscious torment?

By no means do I suggest hell doesn't exist. Hell absolutely exists. It's just not an eternal conscious torment. And there is certainly no glory to be had from sinners burning in it. "What should God, being good, do? . . . It was proper not to have come into being rather than to have come into being to be neglected and destroyed."[35] Better and truer to God's goodness for no human to ever have existed than to be left to their sin, destruction, and eternal torment.

---

31. By choice, pride, and/or by "not accepting the free gift of salvation." Any one or some combination of these is the usual response for folks who believe in eternal conscious torment. For an Orthodox alternative, check out Bradley Jersak's *Her Gates Will Never Be Shut: Hope, Hell, and the New Jerusalem*.

32. Again, See Jersak's *Her Gates* for a beautiful exploration of each biblical term, their use and origins and implications: hell, Hades, Sheol, and Tartarus, as well as a spectrum of descriptions for hell and judgment.

33. 1 Pet 3:19–20.

34. Athanasius, *On the Incarnation*, 66.

35. Athanasius, *On the Incarnation*, 55.

All of that said, hell is very real. It is the force, power, and effect of anything that dehumanizes, takes life, or threatens it. Hell is a daily experience. Hell is addiction winning over recovery. Hell is cancer and chemotherapy and radiation. Hell is a queer kid being kicked out of their home and family for their gender or sexuality. Hell is a war-torn land and babies who died from bomb blasts. Hell is an abusive husband and a partner who feels trapped with no real escape. Hell is mental illness robbing your childhood of an otherwise loving mother.

How does God relate to hell? To addiction? To cancer? To suffering?

To answer these questions, or for any grounded and meaningful conversation about God and God's relationship to suffering and to death, we have to keep in mind that the fullness of God dwelled within and was revealed perfectly in Christ Jesus.[36] This God who so loves as to risk it all, even to lose his own life and be crucified, to watch His Son be put to death, is no stranger to heartbreak and loss and challenge and grief. In the crucifixion, the Father bears witness to the Son's hell, and leaves nothing foreign from His experience. To put it in Trinitarian terms, in the crucifixion there is no aspect or experience of sorrow and loss that is foreign to God. All of it is assumed into the experience of the triune God—the Son who dies, the Father who bears witness, and the Spirit who wails and laments and offers comfort. Not even hell is un-pervaded by God's presence.

The Immaculate Heart

Mary gives us another avenue to experience this sacred kind of solidarity and compassionate *with*-ness that we need. Mary embodies a similar experience to our own: being a fully human parent. She, too, gets what it's like to be able to do nothing but bear witness to her child's suffering. Which feels all too insignificant and, at the same time, all too overwhelming.

---

36. See John 1:1–2 and Heb 1:3.

Mariology

The Immaculate Heart is an artistic representation of this. If you're unfamiliar with it, it's a heart pierced with swords and with fire coming out of the top. Traditionally it is pierced by seven swords for Mary's "seven sorrows," but sometimes it's depicted with three swords or just one. Regardless, the meaning is the same: Mary, the mother of Jesus, bore witness to her Son's suffering—the suffering of her heart and pride and joy.

When Simon's cancer came back after a year of remission I found myself again wrestling with grief and confusion and fear. These all-too-familiar wrestling partners. In wrestling with grief, confusion, and fear I found that they, too, can be portals of prayer when we honestly engage them—though they are never easy or comfortable. As I struggled and wrestled and wondered with these feelings I also wrestled with the existential theological questions of where God was and how God could be good and if God existed at all. During this time the image of the Immaculate Heart kept coming into my mind. I don't entirely know why a lifelong Protestant like me would have this particular image as a recurring mental picture. My best guess is that it is because Mary has been a sojourner with me through a lot, and for a long time.

Despite the image's constant orbit in my thoughts I had to look up what the Immaculate Heart meant. But, if I can be honest, I already intuited it. I knew what it meant before I ever looked it up. I felt it. I know what it's like to be forced to bear witness to your child's suffering, unable to alleviate their pain, to take away the hurt or to put an end to it, or to take it from them and put it on myself try as I might, as if there were some cosmic scales that would require a substitute. I knew the Immaculate Heart's message because it was already my own.

And all I could do was be present. All I could do was be present to Simon and his needs, present to my wife and her needs, present to myself and my needs. All I wanted to do was escape. How desperately I pleaded and prayed for it not to be happening again. But neither escape nor an immediate change in diagnosis were an option. All I could do was witness with my full self. Which feels so powerless, yet it is one of the greatest gifts we can give ourselves.

If you are unfamiliar with the Immaculate Heart, it's such an apt image. A heart pierced and bleeding. A static image. A heart that is full of love, continuing to bleed. Eternally wounded but eternally beating the rhythm of love for the beloved. It is a heart on fire. Radiating and ablaze but not consumed.[37] Every day, somehow, we wake up and continue on. Fueled by love. On fire with God's presence in the midst of our pain, meeting us where we are, even when we don't know it or realize it: "I am with you always."[38]

What is wonderful in the crucifixion, if I may be so bold as to say that, is that we see God is not estranged from suffering. As has been said already, God is precisely in the middle of suffering as a co-sufferer. He has felt his own and is present to us in ours.

What the Immaculate Heart of Mary offers is another dimension—that it is not just that God suffers with us but that there is a fellow human, a fellow sojourner through life and all of life's experiences who knows the particular experience of what it is to watch your beloved child suffer, unable to do anything to alleviate what they are going through. The Immaculate Heart is a symbol of compassionate solidarity. Ours with Mary and Mary's with us.

"Here Is Your Mother"

"'Woman, here is your son.' Then he said to the disciple, 'Here is your mother.'"[39]

As I understand it there are really only two options when you have experienced pain. When your heart breaks the two roads that lay open before us are either to let the experience soften our hearts or to harden them. We will be formed by the pain. That much is a given. The question is in which direction.

---

37. See Exod 3:2.
38. Matt 28:20.
39. John 19:26b–27a NRSVue.

Mariology

I remember a very clear realization that first came on one of those walks after the miscarriages, and again after Simon's initial diagnosis, and a third time after his relapse, that I could let this experience be one that closes me off from others. I could sink into numbing. This, I believe, is the wide road that is easy to find. I could keep relationships at a safe and comfortable arm's distance and never go much deeper than the surface in my conversations and relationships. You can't be hurt if you're not close, right? After all, all of it would be understandable self-preservation, right? I knew I would become an island, and I knew that nobody could convince me that it would be wrong of me. I still think that's true. And for those who might be on that path, I think there is grace for it too. I don't think God is offended when we respond to our hurt in this way. I think God scoops us up into her arms and asks us to show her where it hurts. Be it we realize that in this life or the next.

For me I knew closing myself off wasn't the path I needed. Even if it was at times the one I wanted. Yet I craved a life of flourishing, of community, and of connection with God again—the God whom I wondered might have abandoned me.

I knew I needed to experience healing immediately, here and now, and that it would take the hard work of living in community, of talking and sharing about my experience, to meditate, reflect, and pray. Simon's diagnosis and the psychological shifts it made in my brain are irreversible, so I might as well lean into them and trust that God can be in it too. I might as well trust the thing I've learned to trust thus far: as Richard Rohr says, "Everything belongs."[40] God's love is bigger than our hurt and anger, and can even be found in them.

I believe that option two—the option where we trust God is present to us, is at work within the pain, and is calling us to soften our hearts—is the way Jesus would want for us. As John records

---

40. Fr. Richard Rohr's book *Everything Belongs*, since the time I read it, stands as a favorite. It is the kind of book that shifted a lot for me, and helped me see and experience the kind of faith I had longed for but never knew could exist, that I had thought too good to be true. I can look back and even see me reading that book as a grace of God: God preparing me for whatever comes in life, even childhood cancer.

it, as Jesus is suffering an agonizing death on a cross, he looks and sees his mother and sees John, the beloved disciple. He addresses his mom first—the one who birthed him and bears witness to his sufferings and death—and creates a new kind of kinship between her and his disciple. By the wisdom and love and power that created the heavens and the earth he doesn't let her be alone. He says that she is now kin to John. She is now John's mother and John is her son. Whether he is speaking metaphorically or not doesn't really matter. The point is that they belong to each other. They belong to each other in a way that Jesus wanted to emphasize beyond a shadow of a doubt. When his time was short and his breathing labored he wanted to make sure that this much was clear. In their grief they are not alone.

This is true for us today, too. The words of Jesus, and the heart behind them, speak to us still. There is solidarity with a compassionate, co-suffering God. And there is solidarity with Mary as co-sufferer and as kin.[41] If we choose the path that doesn't close us off to others, we can let our experience be one that catalyzes us to become people who hurt with those who are hurting and to rejoice with those who rejoice.[42] We can hear the Lord's words as if they were spoken to us now, connecting us with all others who hurt, who ache for things to be made right, who want nothing more than for their child's disease to be healed. We can become co-sufferers despite the differences in our experiences. We can become kin, forged in the furnace of love and loss. Jesus' words resonate: "Here is your son. Here is your mother." Christ's words, we come to find, are both a description and prescription. They are a balm for the pains of life. This is what solidarity offers us.

The Christlike way of responding to hurt is to suffer with, to be compassionate. As Paul wrote, "I want to know Christ—to know the power of his resurrection and participation in his sufferings,

---

41. Even liturgically, the yearly journey through Lent culminating in Holy Week and the crucifixion and resurrection is an experience of exactly that: God's compassion and solidarity with us. The Father had to bear witness to the suffering and death of his beloved Son.

42. Rom 12:15.

becoming like him in his death, and so, somehow, attaining to the resurrection from the dead."[43] Experiencing the power of the resurrection—experiencing the with-God kind of life and the power of God that brings even the dead back to life—means we can't shy away from suffering, our own or others.

Franciscan Richard Rohr often says that the two experiences that lead to deep, transformative encounters of God are great love and great suffering. We'd all prefer the first but can't avoid the second. And, in reality, great love necessitates, yet includes and transcends, great suffering. The real question, which makes all the difference, is what do we do in suffering? Do we turn inward and isolate? Or do we turn ourselves outward? Do we heed Christ's words of seeing those who suffer as kin? Do we allow ourselves to be seen vulnerably by others? Do we see the person who suffers as our own mother, as our own son?

There is a world of healing and emancipatory companionship that can be found waiting for us along the way. It does not wait until we meet some final destination, have gone to enough grief meetings, or have come to understand our emotions clinically. Healing comes in the same measure that we are open. When we open a little, a little floods in. When we open a lot, a lot floods in. It's not always easy, but we get out what we put in.

During Simon's treatment he was diagnosed with a transplant-related condition called VOD, or veno-occlusive disease. Essentially, it's a disease that starts in the smallest blood vessels within the liver and, if not stopped, continues to affect larger and larger blood pathways. If not reversed, it is fatal. We learned after the fact from Dr. Saini—once he was well in the clear of VOD and we were talking about finally going home after months in an isolated room within an isolated unit—that his was the second-worst case of VOD that she has seen in her entire career.

Dr. Saini had met with us and told us this in the family room of the bone marrow unit. She breathed the words as though the condition was a physical weight she'd been carrying. At this point we were the only family back there, and it had been that way since

---

43. Phil 3:10–11.

Scarlett had been able to go home about forty days previously. It was the first time since Simon was out of the ICU that she was on service for the in-patient kids. What landed him in the ICU was the fear that his brain was swelling and being damaged by immense levels of ammonia not being filtered out of his blood, which was a condition that came as a result of VOD and another even rarer condition called TMA. Because of the high levels of ammonia in his blood, he was unable to speak—wasn't even really conscious. He could hardly open his eyes, but also wasn't able to rest. He couldn't lay still, rolling and flipping and pulling his NG tube out nightly.

Thank God, as it turned out, his brain wasn't damaged. As they were able to address both conditions his ammonia levels slowly started to trend downward. All that to say, the conversation with Dr. Saini in that family room felt like one where we were all on the other side of something terrifying. We all had just been through hell and were relishing a quiet moment to decompress together.

Dr. Saini is tremendous at making people feel seen, heard, and cared for. That day in particular she must have sat back there and talked with us for an hour. Why? Because that's how much she cares about Simon—and us. She had finished her daily visits with everyone else on the floor so she could spend the extra time debriefing and decompressing with us. The weight of Simon's condition wasn't just on our shoulders.

It becomes very clear talking with Dr. Saini that she possesses an uncanny depth of wisdom. It is wisdom that comes from seeing the impossible happen. It is a wisdom that comes from working with people on the worst days of their lives and on the best days of their lives, knowing that you cannot rush or overlook either. She is a woman who genuinely cares for patients and their families. She does not close herself off, but also maintains a healthy mental separation as best she can so that she can sleep at night and keep doing her job for years to come. And it shows. She balances that razor's edge with wisdom and grace. It shows abundantly in her attentiveness and her care. Dr. Saini is a co-sufferer, and knows the soul-level good that it offers to not be closed off. I don't know Dr. Saini's religious orientation or if she has any claim to any particular faith tradition, but I see Christ in her eyes. I see God in her loving, wise presence.

I can't help but brag on another one of the oncologists on Simon's team: Dr. Hugge. Dr. Hugge was the attending physician when Simon was sent to the ICU. On one particularly frightening and urgent night in the ICU the doctors decided it best to intubate Simon, to do an MRI, and to hook him up to get neurological data all in a whirlwind of precision and decision-making—a feat frankly only possible for an ICU doctor. It is their specialization to make drastic, life-changing decisions on the fly. Dr. Hugge, being alerted as the attending oncologist, rushed back to the hospital at midnight. He met us while we were still in the ICU's waiting room, which we had to go to during the intubation, not that we would want to watch anyway.

Dr. Hugge was obviously shaken up by all that had to happen, and the reasons why, as well as the expediency at which it had to happen. No amount of years can make it an easy situation to be in if you keep your heart open. Living heart-open is like bearing your belly to the world and its woes. It's never easy, and sometimes doesn't even feel worth it, but the Christ-pattern reminds us that it is.

Dr. Hugge isn't exactly the most emotive person. He keeps things pretty close to the chest, betrayed neither by his words nor his nonverbals—things that Mikhaela and I naturally tend to read, but especially came to rely on to be able to sleep at night through Simon's whole journey. As we came to find out, though not emotive, Dr. Hugge is a heart-open kind of person.

Days later when Simon recovered well enough to be transported back to the bone marrow unit, Dr. Hugge came by to see Simon even though he was no longer the attending physician for the in-patient kids that week. He was uncharacteristically happy, unabashedly celebrating Simon's step towards healing. When we saw him Mikhaela and I both teared up, as did he—again, with that kind of knowing that we had all just gone through something enormously terrifying—and we asked if we could hug him. He laughed and obliged. I can't help but believe it did him just as much good to hug us as it did for us to hug him. A simple hug can be one of the most humanizing experiences in such a cold, clinical setting. It centers us back into ourselves, back into our bodies and off of the runaway train of worry and "what-ifs."

When he was leaving I told him I hope he has a much easier and less dramatic week in the outpatient clinic, and he said with a sigh of relief, "Maybe I'll be able to make it to my kid's dive meet this week."

During that hour-long debrief with Dr. Saini, we told her this story, expressing our gratitude for Dr. Hugge showing his softer side. She told us that he is actually the softest one on the team. He works extremely hard at maintaining a professional disconnection because, by wiring, he gets so connected to patients. Of course he does. In his line of work he's been burned; he's co-suffered with parents and patients and it is hellishly painful when kids lose their battles to cancers. And he needs to get up tomorrow and do it all again, because there are kids like Simon who need him. There are parents like Mikhaela and I who need a doctor just like him when their child ends up in the PICU.

I can't speak at all to medical ethics or best practices or job longevity or satisfaction for pediatric oncologists. But what I do know is that that hug meant the world to us. It communicated more than words ever could. For us, what we needed was to grow close to Simon's medical team and to see them as friends. Some of them even have the honorary title of being Simon's aunties (and, by default, they are aunties to Jack, too). It is immensely humanizing to see them not just as people who perform a function, working towards the task of healing our kid, but as people who bear a burden too. They are people who care about us deeply and on personal levels. They are, as much as they can be, in it with us. They are, more than most people are even able to be, in the daily sorrows and celebrations with us, in embodied, incarnational ways.[44] It keeps us and them human. In those liminal moments,

---

44. Looking at you most of all, Sarah.

the humanity in us could recognize the humanity in them, and we went through the cancer journey allowing them to see our humanity. They have seen me cry more than most people in this world, and I feel no shame or remorse about that. I learned with Simon's diagnosis to not stifle my humanity; to not be ashamed to be a person. It is in this humanity that all life and love and dreams and grief and meaning finds grounded-ness. It is in this humanity where Divinity is encountered.

A hug is more than just two people meeting; more than an *I* encountering the idea of a *thou*. We are human and we are so much more than blips in the stories of each other's lives. We are lives overlapped, if even for a brief moment. A hug is two bodies touching. Physically, it's the softest parts of ourselves opening up towards one another. There is a familiarity that is implicated through hugs, a type of intimacy, an embrace. When people get nervous or feel unsettled, we instinctively cover our bellies and our necks, because they are the softest parts of ourselves. In an embrace, we let our bellies be open to one another. Metaphorically, our softest parts can be a safe place for another's softest parts. It is a reminder of our common humanity and of our common experiences. We are co-sojourners through life. We are co-celebrants. We are co-sufferers: "This is *my body*, which is broken for you."[45] "Come, let me hold you for a second." An embrace is the liturgy that consecrates the present moment.

We are human and must bear and grit and rejoice in all that means, and we must do it together. Cain's question to God, "Am I my brother's keeper?," is finally answered with a resounding and resolute "Yes." If even for a brief moment we get to embrace each other in that space—that space of intimates—then we get to recognize the truth of the other's humanity and not shy away from it in ourselves. In a moment like with Simon's doctors it is the reminder of each other's humanity, and that we belong to one another. We are co-sufferers. We are kin.

"'Here is your son.' . . . 'Here is your mother.'"

---

45. See Luke 22:19 and 1 Cor 11:24.

Pneumatology

"Talk about the Spirit must always be contextual.[1] *... The Spirit of God is no general spirit hovering above the cosmos but a Person of the Triune God who indwells believers and creation in specific and tangible ways."*[2]

PNEUMATOLOGY IS THE BIG, theological, seminary word for "the study of the Holy Spirit." The Hebrew word for "spirit" is the word *ruach* and it means, of course, "spirit," but it also means "wind" and "breath" as well. The Greek word *pneuma* is essentially its equivalent. This equivalency means that throughout the Hebrew Scriptures and the New Testament there is a common thread of use and understanding. These words, with their multiple meanings, are an invitation to mystery: to see a world saturated with wonder, beauty, and divine presence. We see a clear example of this conflation in John 20:22 when it says, "And with that he breathed on them and said, 'Receive the Holy Spirit.'" Breath is equated with spirit. Christ's breath is equated with the Holy Spirit. This conflation of breath, wind, and spirit isn't meant to shrink understanding, meaning, beauty, or wonder but to expand them. It is meant

---

1. I hope to convey through this entire project the undercurrent that all conversation about God must be understood to be contextual—both as a hermeneutical framework and as the only real starting place.... We cannot talk about God in a contextless vacuum and never could anyway.

2. Kärkkäinen, *Pneumatology*, 9.

to nuance each definition, to give each a richer texture, a more complex and intricate reality.

The world can be a place where something as simple as the wind or as overlooked as our breath can evoke reflection, understanding, and communion with the divine. Do you want to know what God is like? Sit under some trees. Feel the breeze, watch the way it helps the leaves to sing and dance. Breathe in deeply. God is in all of that.

Who, after all, could capture the mystery of the Spirit of God within any sort of definitive statement? How do you wrangle the wind?

Well, you don't. We can't control the Spirit any more than we can wrangle the wind. The point of life isn't to control the wind as much as it is to learn how to set our sails to it. And the body of religious life is not abstract doctrines—it's to experience the holy wind.

In Acts 2 when the Holy Spirit descends and empowers the apprentices[3] of Jesus, She[4] didn't knock at the door and wait to be invited in.[5] The text says how suddenly the whole house was filled with the sound of a violent wind.[6] Which, personally, I love. It is the sound of a violent wind without the destruction of one. It wasn't a hurricane gale that burst open the door and filled the whole house. It was *like* there was wind. But without the fine china getting blown off the table and the chairs getting knocked over.

---

3. Dallas Willard popularized the contextualized understanding of "disciples" as "apprentices" because it makes more sense in our modern day. We understand what it is to be an apprentice and in an apprenticeship within a certain trade like electrical. John Mark Comer has a wonderful book *Practicing the Way* that is well worth the read and gives practical guidance on how to become apprentices to Jesus.

4. Hebrew and Greek are both gendered languages, much like Spanish and unlike English. *Ruach* and *pneuma* are both gendered as either feminine or gender-neutral. I opt for the more personal feminine.

5. Jennings, *Acts*, 28.

6. Acts 2:2.

Experiences of the holy Spirit can feel like that, don't they? Not violent but inexplicable. Inexplicable but understood. Understood but transcendent.

If by nothing else but by the deepest parts of ourselves. It's an experience that transcends words but is still known, even intuited, on a soul level—like the ancient of days has wired our brains to be able to sense and know God's presence and activity before the frontal cortex ever developed. It is as if we know preconsciously, before language could even shape our thoughts, that in order to have life we must have breath, and our very being cries out for it. We are made for *ruach*.

In my experience it's often as if the knowledge of the all-pervasive, surrounding presence of the Holy Spirit has always been there. This knowledge has resided somewhere deep in the recesses of the most elemental parts of ourselves, and is only uncovered—awakened to. Often, I think it's less that we learn it—as if it's knowledge from outside that we have to be imparted with—and more that we learn language to give shape to what we've already and always known and intuited. It's like some sort of house reno on an HGTV show where the lime-green shag carpet is ripped up to reveal beautiful, century-old hardwood floors original to the house. The wind blew off the dusty, ratty carpet that someone convinced us we absolutely needed in the furniture arrangement of our faith to reveal the beautiful thing that was hidden underneath all along. "The Lord gave and the Lord has taken away; may the name of the Lord be praised."[7]

Experiences with the Holy Spirit are experiences that often move us beyond our language games and break through our logic and rationale. Yet we still *know*. The apostles said it like this: "It seemed good to the Holy Spirit and to us."[8] We can't really always put our finger on *how* we know; we just do.

As a parent of a cancer kid, I know so many other parents who have talked about their kids' initial diagnosis or relapse and say, "I just felt like something was off." I felt the same way when

---

7. Job 1:21b.
8. Acts 15:28.

Pneumatology

Simon relapsed after a year of being in remission. So we assume, whether we say it this way or not, that this is the Spirit of God warning us. As if that will soften the blow.

What's important to keep in mind is that loving parents always carry some amount of worry for their children. It's part of the deal. But once you've already gotten a terrible diagnosis you live in a state of perpetual anxiety. It's hardly a prophetic word. It's trauma. It's not God giving us special insight to anticipate the pain of relapse. It's the simple fact that there isn't a day that goes by that we don't think, *"What if . . ."*

What if this is the last picture I take of them before he gets sick again? What if this is the last walk we go on? What if this is the last time they ever get the chance to eat McDonald's? What if this is the last time I get to kiss her good night?

And then we can almost convince ourselves it's true. Trauma makes it easy to believe that just because it's our fear and our bodies have a physiological response to that fear, then it must be about to happen. Clammy hands and cold sweat are not methods of future-telling. Nor do they actually soften the news of relapse if it happens. I've heard a therapist call it "magic thinking." It's the belief that because we had the thought it's true. It's something like a sign from God beamed straight into my brain. But magic thinking isn't divine. Nor is it real. Trauma isn't prophecy.

There is a big difference between the Spirit's prompting and trauma speaking.

One of those is an awe-inspiring movement of God's presence and activity which is like the sound of the wind filling every nook and cranny of the room of our minds. And the other is an exercise in trying to control the wind. Something like, "If I just anticipate the worst, it won't hurt so bad when (or if) it happens."

What makes it difficult is that the Spirit is a spirit of presence—a spirit of *with*-ness. The Spirit is a spirit of solidarity. The presence of the Holy Spirit is inherently about experiencing the divine here, now, and with us. Parsing out the experience of trauma and the experience of God is an exercise in humility.

Just as I was "sure" that something was wrong when Simon relapsed with his cancer, I've been "sure" a dozen other times that it was back, before and after that. I'm halfway confident every single time I take him to the clinic twice a week. Yet, at this point, he is healthy. He is in remission. These things—that today he is healthy; that today he is in remission; that his bone marrow transplant worked—are what's true. My thoughts don't influence the reality of the situation. Fearful or not doesn't matter. He either is or he isn't in remission. I can't control that. I can't think my way into remission or out of it. I can't be fearful enough that God has pity, nor can I be fearful enough to lessen the pain. All of that is an attempt to control what is ultimately out of our control.

Mikhaela and I regularly have to remind ourselves of what we know is true in the moment: We know from his last appointment that he is doing well. His lab work came back good. His hemoglobin is good; his platelets are good; his ANC is good. Adding insult to injury, usually these fears find more footing at nighttime. As Kate Bowler calls them, it's the difference between our 2 a.m. self and 2 p.m. self.[9] It's become a sort of centering practice, a spiritual practice, to open our monitor app and look at him while saying out loud that he is OK.

It's a practice that has come about naturally like a survival impulse. But I think it's a practice that, when done prayerfully, is an invitation to the Holy Spirit to come fill our house and make her presence known. Of course, "the house" may be literal or proverbial—the house of our mind and heart and soul. Wherever we are dwelling. But, if we're honest, it's a prayer for all of the above. We don't just need God's presence in our mind. We need to feel it all around us like a comforting summer breeze.

Come, Lord Jesus. Send us the comforter. Ease our minds. Help us to get rest.

Do we have our ears tuned to the sound of the wind? Can we feel the breeze as more than just a breeze? Can we turn to our breath and know the *ruach* abides?

---

9. Tippett, "1,107: Kate Bowler," 42:16–43:14.

Pneumatology

As the chapter's beginning quote from Kärkkäinen implies: Pneumatology is an experienced reality. It is not one that sits static, unchanging, and dusty on some theological bookshelf of concepts. It is the *ruach* of God that hovers over the chaos and creates all things.[10]

One of my favorite movies is the Christmas-themed 2019 animated Netflix movie *Klaus*. That's right. I didn't say one of my favorite Christmas movies. It's a favorite movie of mine that also happens to be Christmas related.

At risk of spoiling the movie, the Santa figure—who is much more human than any Santa you've probably ever seen before—you come to find has lost his wife. When she passed, so did the hopes and dreams of what life should be like, and all the plans they made for their shared life together. One of his practices in his solitary life in the wilderness is to carve wooden toys for the children they should have had together if life didn't go the way it did. Relatable feeling, isn't it? The feeling that *this* should never have happened: cancer, a sports career ending torn ACL, a car accident, a failed business, a broken marriage, a miscarriage, a child who doesn't speak to you anymore, addiction, war, poverty, outrageous medical bills, a soul-sucking dead-end job.

Watching the movie you intuit that Klaus continues woodcarving partly as a way to process his grief, partly as a practice in hope, and partly as spiritual practice.[11] More than just toys, he also carves wooden wind chimes that he litters the trees around his cabin with.

Why? Because he has made a practice of listening to the wind. The *ruach* is arguably the main character of this story. His love for his wife and would-be children exists in the wind. There is wisdom from beyond found in the wind. Klaus is a man guided by the wind. Not in the way we may think, as in how we use the phrase "wherever the wind blows," which implies some sort of wayward or laissez-faire attitude. For Klaus the wind serves as a reminder of

---

10. Gen 1:1.
11. Writing this book is exactly all of those things for me.

communion with that which is truer: the eternality of love *and* the action that love compels him to.

Klaus is a man who does not try to wrangle the wind but has learned to set the sails of his life to hear its song. He has made a practice of listening for the wind. He has made an art of the wind and her music.

Next time you're outside and around some trees, listen to the symphony of sound. Birds and squirrels, wind whistling, leaves brushing, and wood creaking—there is music all around, dancing through the air in the power of the *ruach*.

> Concerning the mirror of things
> perceived through sensation,
> we can see God
> not only through them as through his vestiges,
> but also in them
> as he is in them
> by his essence, power, and presence.[12]

Even in the wind; even in our breath.
Even here, even in this, and even now.

Oxygen Masks

We search for divine encounter, for God's transforming presence, not in abstraction but within our lived experiences. What does this mean for those who are facing cancer? Where is the Spirit in it? What does the *ruach* have to do with healing and chemo and surgeries and lumbar punctures?

As anyone who has faced cancer knows—and it's popular lingo around cancer—is that it *feels* like a fight. People often talk about how long someone *fought* cancer or *battled* with it. We use combat imagery. I never really understood until I was in the trenches with my son.

Quite literally, it is chemical warfare within a child's body.

---

12. Bonaventure, *Soul's Journey*, 69.

Pneumatology

We employ powerful chemical agents to kill cells—to eradicate the enemy. And we do this on purpose. The absurdity of the situation is not lost. Life is often beautifully and tragically cruciform: "For the message of the cross is foolishness to those who are perishing, but to us who are being saved it is the power of God."[13] We employ these weapons of destruction directly into the blood of a child for the long-term goal of survival. We do this for the hope of life. It's a damnable situation.[14]

So, again, I ask: Where is God? Where is the Holy Spirit of God? Where is that divine presence in this experience—the one who fills homes and sings in the trees and broods over the chaos like a mother bird to hatch something beautiful, and whose essence, power, and presence are in all things? Because we're terrified to let our son touch the floor; terrified of fevers; terrified of getting woken up in the middle of the night to the sound of him throwing up; terrified the nurse will wake him up at their shift change; terrified of unseen germs carried on the soles of people's shoes.

Our sympathetic nervous system has been on high alert for years now and I don't know if it will ever rest.

Let us come back to Ps 139:

> Where can I go from your Spirit?
> Where can I flee from your presence?
>
> If I go up to the heavens, you are there;
> if I make my bed in hell, you are there.
>
> If I rise on the wings of the dawn,
> if I settle on the far side of the sea,
>
> even there your hand will guide me,
> your right hand will hold me fast.

Even in heaven; even in hell.
Even here, even in this, and even now.
God is in the midst of it. But, again, how? Where?

---

13. 1 Cor 1:18.

14. Not to say that God has damned someone to having cancer. I'd say the exact opposite. I believe God hates cancer. Cancer violates and harms His children and God burns with fury against it.

Not as an abstraction. The psalmist isn't just giving a comforting thought. God is actually here. The *Ruach* is as near as our breath.

For some reason, even throughout Simon's treatments and all the other procedures and interventions he needed, something is particularly haunting for me about low oxygen saturation levels. Perhaps it's my own pneumatology. Perhaps it's something deeply primal and instinctual about knowing the value of clean air. Perhaps it's because the day we found out he likely had cancer he was struggling to breathe, his body so ridden with leukemia that his lung had partially collapsed. Likely, it's all of it.

It's unbelievably difficult to see your kid needing oxygen. The *ruach*—the breath of life—slipping from their being.

I remember one night when Simon was a baby—before his relapse and the bone marrow unit—he was in his third round of chemo treatments. We had a nurse named Taylor that night. Right around shift change his condition turned on a dime. It's a living nightmare for any parent, and is a constantly looming threat on an oncology floor that your child will suddenly turn for the worse. He was fine, playful, and alert, then suddenly threw up. Not just spit up, but projected all of his stomach's contents. Like the flip of a switch, he went from happy and playful to throwing up and feeling miserable. Part of what made this so concerning was that him feeling bad was fairly new. He did so well through his chemo treatments every time. The last time he threw up like that was the day we went to the emergency room and this nightmare of sepsis and cancer began.

This night, hours later, he had multiple visits from the resident doctors and after all of their questions and examinations he was finally able to go to sleep in his hospital crib. As for our own sleep, we were put to ease after watching him be able to sleep. Staring, watching him sleep calmed us down enough to try to get some rest as well. That and trusting Taylor's close watch on him. Feeling safe enough, we tried to get some sleep for ourselves a couple feet away on the pullout couch.

Pneumatology

During the night, his O2 saturation continued to gradually sink lower and lower. Eventually it dipped into the low eighties. Taylor, being the great nurse she is, came in and put an oxygen mask next to his little head, in front of his face. It might seem common practice to give oxygen to someone whose oxygen is bottoming out, but Taylor knew Simon. She knew that she wouldn't just be able to slip an oxygen mask on him. Simon has always been very particular—a truism that his core team learned very quickly. He would never have kept on an oxygen mask. Taylor didn't try to wrestle a sleeping, sick cancer kid to wear an oxygen mask. Instead, she put it in front of his face to "blow by" the oxygen. It bumped his O2 levels from low eighties to the low-to-mid nineties, allowing him and us to get a little more rest. And he had no idea.

That was the Spirit of God. It was oxygen, but it wasn't just oxygen. It was the *ruach* of life. It was the *ruach*. The Spirit is the breath of life.[15]

Isn't that just how the Spirit works?

She doesn't strap us down or wrestle and fight with us but blows past, filling our lungs, sustaining our lives while we don't even know it. Even while we are asleep, literally and figuratively. She rattles the trees and sings through the leaves, whether we notice or not. "This is what the Sovereign Lord says to these bones: I will make breath enter you, and you will come to life. . . . I will put breath in you, and you will come to life. Then you will know that I am the Lord."[16]

If God is everywhere and in all things, as the psalmist and St. Bonaventure (and scores of others) have said, then we should expect God in an oncology room. Which, of course, when you're the one in the oncology room can feel like the furthest thing from reality. But if we learn to listen to the wind, if we set our sails and throw our chimes in the trees of our souls, then we can feel the breeze and hear the sound of the wind speaking to us. We can feel peace enough to rest, to sleep. We can feel peace enough.[17]

---

15. Again, see Gen 2:7 and John 20:22.
16. Ezek 37:5–6.
17. Let me be honest, I certainly didn't always feel peace. Honestly, I would

Bone of My Bone

Bated Breath

Then there are moments that steal your breath. Not like when you are left breathless by the beauty of your spouse, the first cry of a newborn, or a stunning sunset, but the experiences that grip your chest and labor your breathing. That constrict and bind and make you unsure if you can even stand up any longer.

It feels like a Dementor from Harry Potter entered the room.[18] It feels like all the life energy has been sucked out of you, leaving you feeling hollow. In these chest-constricting times where your breathing is shallow you can feel your pulse in your neck, your palms are sweaty, and your stomach is in knots. Hollowness is accompanied by despair and panic. This constriction of my *ruach* has been pretty much a near constant. It was a low-level flame at all times throughout his two bouts with cancer, and the time between.

Mikhaela and I started a practice when we grieved our miscarriages that carried into Simon's treatments. We would intentionally take deep breaths, because we felt that same tight-chested, shallow-breathing feeling all the time. Whether it was our body or our soul craving *ruach* I'm not sure. Probably both.

For whatever reason, we breathed in deep because it just felt like we needed to—as if our bodies knew that we didn't have enough oxygen in our bloodstream, or that we needed to oxygenate our brains, or if for no other reason than to interrupt our disassociation downward spiral and break the cycle of thought we were in.

Secondarily, by grace, it also served as a sign to the other person that we were thinking about the losses, which itself was an invitation and a plea for help out of the spiral of grief. Sometimes the other's deep breath would be a prompt to stop whatever we were doing to talk about it for a while. Sometimes it would be enough to say, "I know," or, "Me too." It was peace enough to know

---

say I hardly did, except for "peace enough." Peace enough to sleep; peace enough to leave the room to bring back food for us; peace enough to shower.

18. Confession: I haven't read all of the Harry Potter books. The scenes from the movies are what I'm picturing here.

Pneumatology

that somebody else was in it with us. It was peace enough to know we weren't alone.

Which is also like the Holy Spirit: to fill in the space and give us what we need to keep going. To be our breath when ours fails.

Jesus told his disciples that when he ascends to the Father he will ask the Father to send another: the Paraclete.[19] Sometimes this word is translated as comforter or advocate. It is how Jesus taught his disciples to expect the Holy Spirit's presence.[20] That she comes as a comforter and advocate.

Paul in Rom 8:26 says, "In the same way, the *Spirit helps us in our weakness*. We do not know what we ought to pray for, but *the Spirit himself intercedes for us* through wordless groans."[21]

"I know." "Me too." These are the words of the Holy Spirit. The Spirit who helps us in our weakness. The Spirit who groans on our behalf when we don't have the words, the breath, or know where to even begin to pray.

"Me too" are the two most powerful words when we're struggling.[22]

How beautiful that the Spirit groans on our behalf. We don't have an impersonal god far off, uncaring, and unmoved. We have one who is in our breath. One who comes to comfort and to advocate. One who says, "Me too," and one who loves us too much to leave us in the pit of despair.

The one who makes it even possible to say, be it now or on some future day, along with the psalmist,

> I waited patiently for the Lord;
>
> he inclined to me and heard my cry.
>
> He drew me up from the desolate pit,
> out of the miry bog,
> and set my feet upon a rock,
> making my steps secure.

19. See John 14:16; 15:26; 16:7.
20. John 14:26.
21. Emphases mine.
22. Brown, "Listening to Shame," 18:46–19:10.

Bone of My Bone

> He put a new song in my mouth,
> a song of praise to our God.
> Many will see and fear
> and put their trust in the Lord.[23]

Be it now or in the next life, eventually we will all say, "He drew me up from the desolate pit. . . . He put a new song in my mouth, a song of praise to our God." And I know of nobody in my life who could hope so prophetically and so daringly like this as a child with pediatric cancer. There's no strength like a kid on an oncology floor.

Recently, Addi, a young girl who also had a bone marrow transplant at the same hospital Simon did, passed away after a long, courageous fight against cancer. When her mom posted on Facebook to let family and friends know of Addi's transition into God's embrace, she shared Addi's words: "No matter what, Mom, Jesus is on the other side of this thing."

Lord Jesus, send the comforter. Send the advocate.

Chances and Control

When Simon was in remission the first time we felt safe enough to ask his primary oncologist what the chances were that Simon got diagnosed with leukemia.

From the research and statistics at the time, she told us that between 10,000 and 12,000 kids in the USA are diagnosed with cancer every year. Half of those, between 5,000 and 6,000, are diagnosed with some kind of leukemia. And only 1 percent of *those* kids are infants. Meaning only 50–60 kids. One of 50. Out of all the babies in the country, he was one of 50. This isn't even to narrow it down further to how many infants are diagnosed with the specific kind of leukemia that he was diagnosed with.

What are chances? What are statistics? Surely you can understand when I say that statistics mean nothing to me anymore.

---

23. Ps 40:1–3 NRSVue.

Pneumatology

Things either happen or they don't. Being one of 50 babies diagnosed with leukemia will shatter any notion of safety, chances, statistics, and predictability.

What's been almost equally as wild to learn is how non-specific medicine is. I used to be under the impression that medicine is a very black-and-white sort of thing: you have a bacterial infection, so you take an antibiotic, then the bacterial infection is eliminated. A+B=C. I naively assumed all of medicine worked this way: find the right combination of drugs or medication and you will have good outcomes.

It wasn't until well into Simon's first round of chemotherapy that I learned that chemotherapy doesn't always work. It wasn't until he needed a stem cell transplant that I learned about HLA typing and how you can do a successful transplant without being a perfect match, but also how a perfect match doesn't even guarantee success.

How much of science is best-laid plans made with crossed fingers. How much of life.

With bone marrow transplants there are three ways of extracting stem cells. They can draw peripheral blood, meaning the blood is taken out of the arm much like a normal blood donation you'd expect from the Red Cross.[24] Stem cells can also be drawn out through the hip bones.[25] The National Marrow Donor Program (NMDP, previously known as Be The Match) will fly candidates from around the world and pay for all the costs associated with the procedures with this type of donation. As well, we have been told about the NMDP connecting adult donors with adult recipients so they can meet as well. The third option for getting stem cells

---

24. If you're able, please consider donating blood, platelets, and plasma as often as possible. Simon went through multiple bags, sometimes multiple different blood products, in a single day. The Red Cross is always in desperate need of more donations.

25. Please also consider registering as a bone marrow donor through NMDP, previously known as Be The Match, but still accessible through bethematch.org.

for a bone marrow transplant is through donated umbilical cord blood.[26] This is the type that Simon received.

We don't know anything really about the donor except that she is a girl who is only weeks apart in age from Simon. While it just so happened that his donor was also around two years old at the time, properly stored cord blood can be saved for around twenty years.

Stem cells from umbilical cord blood are ideal. It's the best option because the stem cells are essentially the most malleable. Practically speaking, they have the highest success rate of engraftment, which, in turn, means a successful transplant. They are also least likely to cause problems because they haven't really had years to grow accustomed to a certain body, so the chance of graft-versus-host disease (GvHD) is also lower. However, umbilical cord blood is really only for children, especially those that weigh less than 70 kilograms, or 150 pounds, due to the limited sample size—you can't just get more cord blood if you need it the way you can stick an adult's hip again if needed.

Be it from the suggestion of an OBGYN, a midwife, the hospital's policy, or their own personal experience, for some reason some family around the same time that we had Simon gave the expressed permission to publicly bank their baby's cord blood. We don't know the family, their names, nor will we ever—the NMDP doesn't do connections when it's cord blood for the safety of the child.

I don't know what those odds are that they made that decision. Was it policy or a hard-earned lesson from a family tragedy? I can never know. But what I can choose to trust is that the Spirit was at work however it happened. Whether it was making life come from a hardship the family faced, or set in place years before in the hospital's default policy, or because of a nurse's guidance, or because the family just thought it sounded like a good

---

26. If you or someone you know is pregnant or plan to be, please consider talking to your OBGYN or midwife about donating your umbilical cord blood. And donate in a public bank. They have clearer regulations that they have to follow. A family in the unit with us had issues with a private bank because they weren't able to confirm adequate storage and handling for months.

idea—whatever the reason I can choose to believe that the Spirit had her hand in the process.

It's a different kind of trust to choose to believe what is ultimately unknowable, like the reason why that family donated their daughter's umbilical cord into the public bank.[27] Some things are best believed in not because it changes any outcome, but because it changes us for believing in them. How? Because the object of our trust isn't a specific outcome, or feeling certain, or knowing facts. Choosing this kind of trust—that the Spirit of God is at work in all times and for all good—changes us, because the object of our trust is nothing else but the *ruach* of God. And how often the Holy Spirit invites us into this kind of transfiguring trust.

The Spirit invites us to trust in her movements, guidance, and love more than statistics. Statistics are comforting because they are more controllable. We can make decisions based on statistics, minimize risks based on odds, maximize profits and bottom lines based on data. And they *feel* more controllable, which, in turn, is what gives us great comfort. It feels as though everything is kept in our power. It makes us feel like the pioneers of our own lives, the masters of our own destinies. It plays into the very American, yet very misguided, notions of pulling yourself up by your bootstraps and that working hard always equates with financial success. Insurance claims and our entire market economics are based on statistics. Stocks are bought and sold with the odds in mind.

What cancer reveals is that all of that is an illusion. Control is an illusion. Chances are ultimately meaningless in the things that are ultimate. Things happen or they don't. Control is a comforting illusion at times, sure, but a shadow nonetheless. It is vapor.[28] When Jesus was tempted by the devil in the desert, each temptation was

---

27. We have friends we made from the oncology floor that had issues with private banks not being able to guarantee they followed all of the safety precautions. Public banks, to my knowledge, have to be more transparent about their processes due to governmental regulations.

28. See Eccl 1:2.

a temptation to control something.[29] Yet, empowered by the Holy Spirit, he denied each temptation.

In the world where we buy and sell on shadows, where we ascribe worth and value to vapor, what if the greatest gift the Spirit offers us is an invitation to trust something more than our own control?

Try as I might and despite how often I wish I could, on this side of the diagnosis I can never imagine buying into the illusion of control like I did before. Everything now feels like it comes with an asterisk. Vacation plans are set, unless . . . We will celebrate holidays in the usual fashion, unless . . . We can count on a daily rhythm, unless . . .

Nothing is ever actually set. Nor does it feel like it is. Not anymore. The fragility of life cannot be unlearned. Of course, a cancer diagnosis is an extreme version of this, but we all have little versions of these moments all the time. When we get a stomach bug we are taken out for days. How can a tiny virus that we can't even see incapacitate us for so long? Our work, our weekends, our vacation plans, or whatever else are called off. You might tear a muscle in your shoulder or a tendon in your knee and all of a sudden you realize how your beloved body is aging and you can't quite move like you used to. More than ever you probably now recognize how often those muscles or ligaments are used, unnoticed, and unappreciated. When one nostril is clogged we wish we could remember what it's like to breathe unobstructed. Our imaginations are arrested to the present moment, the present reality, the present fragility of our mortal lives and bodies. Then, something as existentially shaking as a life-threatening condition is like this but compounded all the more.

We can't go back to what "normal" was before. Like the famous line: "No man ever steps in the same river twice, for it's not the same river and he's not the same man."[30]

I certainly never have been able to step back into the river of "normal life" as I once did. Instead, a new normal is born. I can

---

29. See Matt 4:1–11.

30. The ancient Greek philosopher Heraclitus is attributed with this line.

never unknow what I now know, unsee what I've seen. And part of what I now know is that control is an illusion. Which is terrifying. But it could also be liberating. I believe that it is exactly in this space that God is at work inviting us into that deeper, transfiguring trust.

It can be wildly freeing to come to understand that life is not in my power. I am dust, here today and gone tomorrow.[31] But there is a power that does hold all things together.[32] I don't have to hold it all together. I can be brave enough to be vulnerable.

I get to fall apart.

Life with God is an ongoing exercise in learning to trust—to trust the one who created, sustains, and will restore all things—and to be transformed the more we trust.

What Is Essential?

There's a reason that God gives the name "wrestles with God" to His people. It's not because people are obstinate, prideful, or arrogant. Though these admittedly do come too easily. It's because to be in a relationship with God is to wrestle with God. "Wrestles with God" is not a negative description but a sacred moniker.

God knows it to be holy business. God knows that to wrestle is ultimately about control. Who is in control of the situation? God is aware how much we like control, how accustomed to its allure we are, how much we've come to depend upon and crave it. God knows how grasping for control is the primordial sin of humanity. "The fall" of humanity comes from the temptation to "be like God."[33] He sees how we plan and build our nests and our bank accounts and our retirement plans and how we expect eighteen-year-olds to decide the trajectory of their lives. Our entire social systems and psyches—collective and personal—have been constructed around the artifice of control.

---

31. For a power reflection on this, please go and listen to the "Vapor (A Meditation)" by The Liturgists.
32. See Col 1:17.
33. Gen 3:5.

Bone of My Bone

But God wrestles us out of this hell.

The wrestling itself is a blessing. And through the wrestling we are blessed. Just like the story of Jacob who wrestled with God.[34] He walked with a limp for the rest of his life, but he was blessed. The tragedy in this would be to mistake the limp for a curse, or an unfortunate accident, or side effect of wrestling with God. The limp is part of the blessing. A type of daily sacrament. It is being forced to slow down, even to practice Sabbath: to rest and see how the world keeps spinning and life keeps teeming. If Jacob understood his limp as a gift, we can't know. But, as has been said already, we can choose to trust it to be a gift. We can choose to trust that God really does work all things together for good.[35] As seems to be the norm of life, though, it seems like it takes a long time before we can look back and see the gift amidst the hardship.

What we do know about Jacob, though, is that he was forced to slow down. To not rely on his own power. To take it day by day, and moment by moment. He is certainly not the same person he was just the day before.

That all sounds just like living in a hospital.

Hospital time is infinitely slower than time outside of the hospital. It's an existential necessity to take it all day by day, regularly even hour by hour. This is especially true when the shortest possible in-patient stint is twenty-eight days.[36] To wake up is to step into the ring to wrestle again with God. Every day, even every moment, is a wrestling with the Spirit. It's perpetually exhausting with no reprieve in sight. And not just physically exhausting—though it is that. It's a soul-level exhaustion. A constant mental fatigue. I've never been so exhausted for so long.[37]

---

34. Gen 32:22–32.

35. Rom 8:28.

36. Simon's diagnosis of AML with its aggressive treatment required such long planned stays. Other cancers, like ALL for example, typically only have planned stays as long as a week.

37. Even when we could have someone come and watch Simon for a couple hours so we could leave and spend time just Mikhaela and me, it never was exactly restful or energizing. Our bodies were elsewhere but our spirits were still on the oncology floor. Such disembodied living never can give us the respite

Pneumatology

Seventy days in-patient was an eternity, yet seventy days at home came and went without notice. Seventy days in an isolated bone marrow unit is an absurd experience. What's really strange is that each unit in a hospital has its own gravity. Time moves differently on each floor. For instance, time is measured differently on an oncology floor than in the intensive care unit. In oncology, time and trends are measured over days, even weeks. You have to plan to be in it for a long haul. In the ICU, though, time is measured in minutes, even seconds. Every second is crucial to stop a brain from swelling, or blood loss, or organ failure. When Simon needed to move from the bone marrow unit to the ICU it was a disorienting experience. A temporal vertigo. Time swells and shrinks; is keen and obtuse. But it's not just adjusting to hospital time that is bewildering.

You are forced to not rely on your own power. You have to work alongside a team of nurses and doctors. You're forced to take it day by day because of the enormity of it all. Jesus' words aren't just sage advice, they are a necessity. They are reality: "Therefore do not worry about tomorrow, for tomorrow will worry about itself. Each day has enough trouble of its own."[38]

And, of course, each of these things—the loss of the illusion of control, the vertigo of relation to time, and being forced to rely on power that is not yours—changes you deeply. You are never the same after a life-altering diagnosis as you were before. It calls into question and challenges and changes your values, your priorities, your rhythms, your habits, your philosophies and theologies and worldviews. It is a traumatic experience that wounds every dimension of who you are. Like Dr. Bessel van der Kolk wrote, "We have learned that trauma is not just an event that took place sometime in the past; it is also the imprint left by that experience on mind, brain, and body. This imprint has ongoing consequences for how the human organism manages to survive in the present. Trauma results in a fundamental reorganization of the way mind and brain

we need.

38. Matt 6:34, but it's worth reading verses 25–34.

manage perceptions. It changes not only how we think and what we think about, but also our very capacity to think."[39]

It is a crucible and it will change you. I'm not saying cancer is a blessing. Certainly not. But I do believe the clarity it brings to life can be. Again, the question is *how*. As we've been building towards, I think the answer to that question lies in how much we hold on to the illusion of control.

By no means am I suggesting to not ask your doctor questions or advocate every waking hour for your child. That is about all the power you do actually have. Use it. God gave you a certain kind of power for you to exercise. Nobody else knows your kid like you do. And nobody loves your kid like you.

But we cannot control outcomes, statistics, or chances anymore than we can control the weather. All that we can control is ourselves, and, even then, we don't have total control.[40] What we can control is our openness to the Spirit.

The Spirit will teach us in accordance to the degree to which we let ourselves remain open to our experiences.

Sometimes what we need for the day is to numb or distract ourselves. But if done as a rule rather than an exception then we teach ourselves to instinctively shut off parts of ourselves. Ultimately we numb ourselves to life in all its parts. Like Brené Brown has said: "You cannot selectively numb emotion. You can't say, here's the bad stuff. Here's vulnerability, here's grief, here's shame, here's fear, here's disappointment. I don't want to feel these. . . . When we numb those, we numb joy, we numb gratitude, we numb happiness."[41] We become desensitized across the board. We numb not only the hard emotions but also our openness to life's beauty and splendor. We numb ourselves to the presence and solidarity of God. We numb ourselves from connection to others—to our

---

39. Van der Kolk, *Body*, 21.

40. We can't control our emotions, per se, only the actions we take from them. We can't control our heartbeats or our kidney function. We can't control our biases, our habits, or even our knee-jerk reactions—we have to intentionally and methodically retrain them if we want to do differently. This is the entire premise of spiritual formation. For a biblical reference, see Rom 7:15.

41. Brown, "Power of Vulnerability," 15:36–16:38.

spouse or partner, to our medical team, to the unique community and communion that can be formed on an oncology floor.

Far from being just the opposite to habitual numbing, choosing and remaining open to all of it is the antidote. In my life, I have never been healed by numbing, but I have had healing conversations with friends who would go on walks with me. I've never been saved by being selective with what emotions I allow myself to feel, but I have found freedom in recognizing each one as it comes. On the days the scariness of Simon's cancer made me an atheist, I was held by the faith of Mikhaela. The wind is whispering in all of these.

In our attentive openness we don't just remain open to what the Spirit is doing, or to all of our emotions, but we can learn to focus on the things that matter most in life. We can be blessed with the epiphany that we don't really have time for the things that we used to spend so much time striving for. For me it looked like coming face-to-face with and shattering my idol of control, an ego-fueled self-image, renegotiating my value placed in societal notions of success and power like money, status, and prestige. I used to feel undervalued at my church because I wasn't paid "enough." But, when I'm honest with myself, "enough" was always a moving target. I figured, as is the American way, you show value by how many dollars you're willing to put towards something. If I was valued more, I would be paid more. But after the long, deconstructing journey of cancer, these things have been uncoupled for me.

The things that used to concern us so much can be rightly seen in their proper respect as just *things*. Not that they don't have any importance or aren't worth any of our attention, but that they certainly aren't worth our stress and anxiety.

Emails and work and the world all keep spinning even if I don't respond, or if I'm not in the meeting, or if I don't answer the phone call. We are not essential. Zoom out and you can see that the birds in Tanzania are unaffected because you had to stay home sick. Your coworkers are just fine even though you took a vacation. Life thrives and abounds even when you miss the email about the Zoom call. We are not essential. We were not created to produce for Pharaoh or to accumulate for ourselves. We are not essential. Except, of course, where we *are* essential.

We were created in, through, and for relationships.

When Simon was a baby and was just diagnosed, our heads still reeling and ears still filled with the ringing of our world's being blown up, we met one of the doctors who would be on his oncology team: Dr. Bhatla.

When she was leaving Simon's room, she stopped, looked at him again, and smiled softly. "It's clear that you love him very much." Turning towards us with that same soft smile she said, "Love will help him through this."

Existential crises like the experience of cancer have a way of revealing to us, if we let them, where we actually are essential and what is actually essential to us. It shows us where our hearts are. They have the power to reveal to us the things that God has called us to do specifically—the little slice of kingdom work within our contexts given our gifts, personality, and skills.

Love doesn't cure or prevent cancer. It doesn't stop bankruptcy or foreclosure or hurricanes or water main breaks. But it keeps us connected. Love keeps us open. It keeps hope alive and looks like being welcomed back home when we've lost our house. It looks like the coast guard searching everywhere for survivors. Love looks like paying the bills of pediatric cancer families. Love looks like the nurses and doctors and hospital staff who chose to go to work today and willingly step into the hell of childhood cancers.

As much as we wish we could, we couldn't fight Simon's cancer. His body, the chemo, the doctors, and the nurses had to do that. But we could make damn sure he never felt alone. We could fight for each other against the feelings of fear, of isolation, of despair, of the unknown. We could love Simon. And we could love those who are taking care of us. We could fight the impulse to close ourselves off. We could resist from seeing his care team just as people who perform a function. We could love people we just crossed paths with. We chose to love and keep our hearts open to families in the elevator; for the families carrying their kid rushing into the emergency room; for the patients brought on the helicopter. We chose to love Keith in the cafeteria. We love Linda, the custodian. We love Sarah who saved Simon's life, and, yet, is still somehow an even better friend than she even is a nurse.

Not much is different than an open heart and a heart of prayer. If there is any difference at all. An open heart, a heart of prayer, choosing to love are one and the same reality. Practically, for us, it meant we chose to love all of these people God has blessed us with—these people we get to cross paths with today.

And so we did. We do.

That is all we could control. That was what was in our power. That is where we are essential: in our relationships; to the people around us.

Christology

> *"The way for Christians to enter into the mystery of and relationship with God is through Christology."*[1]

> *"Remember Christ has no human body now upon the earth but yours; no hands but yours; no feet but yours. Yours, my brothers and sisters, are the eyes through which Christ's compassion has to look upon the world, and yours are the lips with which His love has to speak. Yours are the hands with which He is to bless men now, and yours the feet with which He is to go about doing good through His Church which is His body."*[2]

TO TALK ABOUT CHRISTOLOGY is to also talk about incarnation—that the Word became flesh.[3] "God with us."[4] Incarnation is the first and most foundational aspect of Christology. It is the God-drawn-near revelation. It is the light by which all the rest is seen. If Christology has anything to offer, it must meet us in our humanity. Divinity must be inextricably linked to humanity to have any merit. Any theology that says God is distant, uncaring, uninvested,

---

1. Niles, *Doing Theology*, 17.
2. Pearse, *British Friend*, 15.
3. John 1:14.
4. Matt 1:23.

or unmoving isn't worth our time or adoration. God must be in this. Or else nothing really matters, even God.

To reuse the James Cone quote from the introduction of the book: "Christianity begins and ends with the man Jesus—his life, death, and resurrection. He is the Revelation, the special disclosure of God to man, revealing who God is and what his purpose for man is."[5]

I waste no time on a shallow incarnation that purports that the fullness of God dwelled in Christ Jesus two thousand years ago yet is no longer with us in the world today. The Christological claim of the incarnation is of a deep incarnation. It is the claim that even beyond the historically bound human person, the fullness of Christ himself is with us in real, tangible ways today, which is implored to us when we take Jesus' words seriously: "On that day you will realize that I am in my Father, and you are in me, and I am in you,"[6] and, "Surely I am with you always, to the very end of the age."[7] What else does he mean when he takes bread and wine and says that it is his body and blood?[8]

He must surely mean that he is always and unceasingly with us and in us. Nothing short of that will do.

No Body But Yours

I saw Christ crucified, and, in the same instant, I saw the power of his resurrection.

I saw Christ on October 30, 2023. It wasn't the first time, but I had never seen this side of him before. His blood was A positive and there was a tiny 67 mL volume of him, containing 45 mL 5 percent Albumin in Dextran. This was the day Simon received his bone marrow transplant: "Day 0."

---

5. Cone, *Black Theology*, 34.
6. John 14:20.
7. Matt 28:20.
8. Luke 22:19 and 1 Cor 11:24.

Christ's cross fashioned into an IV pole. His blood flowed by nothing but gravity pulling it out of the bag. The speed of God is a slow drip. No machine, no pump to regulate the speed of flow. This isn't a regular blood infusion. Just Christ and God's intricate and good creation of gravity working together in life-saving synergy: the divine and the divine's creation working in harmony.[9]

Christ didn't just get wheeled into the room on October 30, but had been at work, had been present, before that holy day, too. Christ is the little girl whose umbilical cord blood was used to heal Simon. Christ is the parents who chose to donate it. Christ in the hospital staff at her birth. Christ in the OBGYN who followed the strict yet proper protocol to collect, handle, and ship the cord blood safely. Christ in the transport teams to carry the stem cells. Christ in the weather and road conditions to allow for safe transport. Christ in the ones who processed the sample. Christ in the ones who froze it. Christ in Simon's team who chose that specific sample. Christ in Simon's nursing and doctoral staff. The deep incarnation of Christ everywhere, in all things.

Christ in the marrow.
Christ has no umbilical cord but yours.
Christ has no bone marrow but yours.
Christ has no stem cells but yours.

Christ, the Born One

Each of the Gospels have such beautiful differences. Their tones, their writing styles, their emphases—you get clearly that they are different people writing from different perspectives to different people and for different reasons. John's Gospel, for example, is very cosmic. It begins with the Word (Greek: *Logos*). The creative,

---

9. What would it look like to see and believe this all the time? Surely we would come to a place of "considering the lilies" (Matt 6:28) and realize that the rains of grace fall on the just and the unjust (Matt 5:45). We would have a faith that is deeply ecological. We would understand that we are not separate from creation but part of it. We would be able to hear the birdsong and know it too is worship.

Christology

designing, sustaining, unifying force or logic, who is God and was with God in the beginning.[10] John's is a very big picture, pulled back to emphasize the divine nature of Jesus.

What I love about Luke's Gospel is the raw materiality of it. It's earthy. It's practical and challenging. Jesus in Luke's Gospel continues to rail against things like money and empire. Luke puts Jesus in his larger historical context, so Luke starts the Gospel account before Christ is even born. Jesus isn't born until the second chapter. This raw and gritty Gospel is likewise full of wonder and anticipation. It is very clear from Luke's Gospel account that Jesus was "born of a woman and the Hebrew gene pool."[11]

More than just taking one or another, I love that the biblical witness is to receive all of them together. The cosmic Word, nurtured by Mary's body. The cosmic Word, unable to hold his own head up. The cosmic Word, completely dependent on two new parents for everything. The cosmic Word, who pooped and spat up and nursed at his mother's breast and cried in the middle of the night waking his parents up.

The cosmic Word who was carried in his mother's belly for nine months. The cosmic Word who was sustained by an umbilical cord. The cosmic Word who had to learn language and pronunciation and turn-taking in conversation. The cosmic Word who had to learn to say "please" and "thank you."

The cosmic Word who has shown up again. This time not being sustained by an umbilical cord but saving another through one.

I don't think the cord blood became Christ. It was always Christ. It was Christ when the little girl who was nourished by it was still attached to it. It was Christ when it was clamped. It was Christ when it was cut: "This is my body given for you" (Luke 22:19). It was Christ when it was donated. It was Christ when it was frozen. It was Christ when it was received. "The Crucified one is the form of God's participation in history!"[12]

---

10. John 1:1–2.
11. Toolan, *At Home in the Cosmos*, 206.
12. Koyama, *Water Buffalo Theology*, 57.

If we can receive the presence of Christ and be nourished and sustained by Christ in the elements of Communion, then we can surely also receive Christ and be sustained by Christ through the lifeblood of our bodies. "By his wounds we are healed."[13] To donate blood, plasma, platelets, or stem cells is to preside over the Eucharist.

Desert

Living a slow, simple, humble life is usually a forced hand. Hardly anybody chooses it. It's often thrust upon us, forced by the strings of fate. It is a way of life from which we would all rather return to self-important things. We would rather cling to the old gods. Pride, purpose, production, and hustle. We would just as soon worship again at the altars of the illusions of our own control and power over the things that matter most—even over the things that don't. Too often we assume that to be human means to exert force. It is to bend things to our will.

I've since come to believe that to be human is to be able to be changed, not to exert change on others.

The biblical imagery for this forced hand is the desert. Whether it's with the Israelites in the exodus or Jesus in his temptation, it's clear that the desert is not the place you want to be but is the place that will transform us if we allow it. That is, if we don't submit to the temptation to build new idols. One thing is clear in the desert: there is no going back. The Red Sea is closed. There is no going back to a "before." Have you had this experience before? You cannot unsee what you have now seen, can't unknow what is now known, can't take away the experience you have now had.

Life in the desert is inherently a time of lack. It is a supreme awareness of what is not—particularly of what is not but should be. There is no air conditioning, no water, no reprieve. There is no shade to rest in, no escape from the relentless assault of the sun's heat. There is no balm for our scorched skin or our weary bodies.

---

13. Isa 53:5.

Christology

The desert may be internal. It could be a spiritual wrestling you've had. It could be a coming-out experience. It could be a relationship. It may be the disorienting loss of one. It might have been something you went through, and it might be something you carry with you. Sometimes, it can be linked to a specific place. Maybe it's something you're going through right now. For many it's probably some combination of any or all of the above. For us, the hospital clinic is a draining place. We love the people and treasure the relationships we've formed with Simon's team. But a couple-hour visit is physically, emotionally, and mentally taxing. When I get home I crash on the couch. Sometimes on the way home I will cry just to acknowledge and express the emotions that flooded in me.

During one visit I mentioned the feelings of anxiety and exhaustion after clinic visits to Simon's oncologist, Dr. Saini, when she asked how I was doing. She's the kind of person that genuinely cares when she asks. She asks to invite, yet never forces, more than the pat answer everyone expects: "Good. How are you?" She was the first person to tell me how trauma can be linked to a specific place, and that just by going back to that same physical location—even under much different circumstances—can trigger a body's trauma responses.

Like said previously, time moves differently in the hospital. The center of gravity inside versus outside of the oncology floor is wild. Aside from the trauma stored in the body, part of that is because every day can look like the last, and another part of that is because the measurements and markers are different than I ever expected. When Simon was recovering from veno-occlusive disease (VOD), his bilirubin would crawl down by 0.4 from one day to the next then back up 0.2 the following day; down 0.2 then up 0.3. If you looked at the day-to-day it often seemed as if it was going nowhere—sometimes even like his condition was worsening. But the reality, as his oncologists and nurses kept reminding us, was the larger trends. What were last Monday's levels compared to this Monday's levels? What have the levels done over the last thirty days? It's exhausting and dreadful. You are learning a new medical language and learning a new relation to time. It's draining and disorienting and, because it's a life-or-death scenario, it is full of fear and despair.

Time is at a near standstill. One day looks like the last. Days blur. Sense of time is crushed under the weight of fear and angst. "How long, Lord? Will you forget me forever? How long will you hide your face from me? How long must I wrestle with my thoughts and day after day have sorrow in my heart? How long will my enemy triumph over me?"[14]

It's hard to live a slow life. It's hard to live a simple life. It's hard to live a life that has been laid low. I craved control and to stay busy, to numb and to fill my schedule. But cancer brings with it a simple life: a life that is stripped of the slag.

Which is also, and paradoxically, exactly why the desert can be our greatest teacher. Life in the desert is a life in which all that is left is a clarity of what really matters. It is with the power of reality that Christ taught, "Blessed are the poor in spirit, for theirs is the kingdom of heaven. Blessed are those who mourn, for they will be comforted. Blessed are the meek, for they will inherit the earth."[15] And that's exactly what you are on an oncology floor: poor in spirit, mournful, and meek.

Life on the oncology floor is like being thrust out into the desert. Exiled from the land of self-important pride, of inflated purpose, of illusions of control and power. But the good news is that Christ is in the desert, too.

Christ is familiar with the arid, barren landscape of a soul in the desert: "My God, my God, why have you forsaken me?"[16] Those are not the words of someone unfamiliar.

In Christ's presence—be it found in stem cells or hemoglobin or nurses or custodians—we can come to see that the desert is filled with the presence of God. The one who gives manna for daily bread goes with us. God abides, providing sustenance in whatever form it may come that day, nourishing some aspect of our humanity.

14. Ps 13:1–2.
15. Matt 5:3–5.
16. Matt 27:46.

Christology

It's no wonder, then, why the early church's wise teachers lived in the desert. They didn't live in the desert because they were sagely. They became wise because of their simple way of life. The desert is the site of incarnational wisdom. They went through great challenges and sufferings and met God in them. Thomas Merton cites the Desert Fathers: "one of the elders said: Poverty, tribulation, and discretion . . . if these three actions are found in a man, then God dwells in him."[17]

There is no escaping these experiences in a cancer ward. They are the air we breathe. The desert of an oncology floor is a place of spiritual, mental, and emotional poverty. It is the sight of tribulation after tribulation. It is the ground zero of discretion, humility, and frailty.

Life on the oncology floor is being thrust out of the comfort of life as it should be, of life as it was planned, of life as it was hoped for and into the desert. It is a falling into the loving arms of a loving God. God is found in Hades, too.[18] But it is falling nonetheless.

These three—poverty, tribulation, and discretion—are part and parcel of living in the desert, but they can be learned to be internal postures as well. Instead of mere afflictions, they can be our teachers for navigating life.[19] To say it one way, instead of the desert taking us captive, we can take the desert captive and submit it to Christ.

Instead of being beholden to money and success, we can learn from the desert to internalize a life free of these trappings. We can be a people of immense charity, of overflowing abundance in the things that matter. We can be rich not in accolades and pats on the back and letters behind our names but in the success of

---

17. Merton, *Wisdom of the Desert*, 26.

18. Psalm 139:8—*Sheol* being the land of the dead. *Hades* is the Greek equivalent. Psalm 139 doesn't imagine a separation of heaven and hell as two separate places like Dante dreams up in his *Inferno* in the medieval period, which has dominated our religious and societal imagination since. For the psalmist, the land of the dead is the land for all of the dead. Christ is even in this hell.

19. Which is the cruciform nature of God. To take even the worst and to make it teem with life.

deep, healthy, and fulfilling relationships. "Blessed are you who are poor, for yours is the kingdom of God."[20]

Instead of being beholden to security, comfort, and control, we can learn from the desert to internalize a life free of these illusions. We can be a people of gratitude: expressing thankfulness for every moment we get with our loved ones, that we got to eat breakfast that day, thankful for the smile of a stranger. "Blessed are those who mourn, for they will be comforted."[21]

Instead of beholden to pride, systems of domination, and power struggles, we can learn from the desert to embody a life that is joyful. Joy is not happiness, but a deep abiding trust that "all shall be well, and every manner of things shall be well," as Julian of Norwich famously wrote.[22] We can be a people with a persistent joy that finds its rest in the goodness of a loving God who is always drawing near. "Blessed are the pure in heart, for they will see God."[23]

I know of no wiser teachers in the desert than Simon's nurses. Theirs is a wisdom that only comes from experience. It is a wisdom that comes from suffering, from a co-suffering kind of loving presence. It is hard-won wisdom.

Honestly, more tangibly than in any other place, Christ is in those nurses. The nurses are the wise sages of life in the desert of the oncology floor. They are the Desert Mothers and Fathers. They seem to know the words you need when you need them. They know the layout of the sand, the way to carve out space for the crucial need of respite. They know the wisdom to make it one day at a time in a vast, disorienting landscape almost bereft of hope.

This is not to say that they might as well be monks and nuns with how virtuous they are. If for no other reason, they are Christ's hands because they serve. They spend hours each week entering into the deserts of other people's lives. Many they witness on the best days of their lives, and many on the worst days of their lives.

20. Luke 6:20.
21. Matt 5:4.
22. Julian, *Revelations of Divine Love*, 20.
23. Matt 5:8.

They have seen more kids pass away than anyone should. Yet, still, they persist in their mission of being a loving presence, and in their serving they imitate the Christ-pattern. They make themselves lowly and change bedsheets and bedpans. They give their life's precious few hours for the sake of others. Every day they face little deaths and witness little resurrections. Theirs is an incarnational vocation. By saying "Yes" to serving—to dedicating twelve hours a day to helping, serving, and saving lives—they are, in turn, saying "Yes" to God's activity in the world.

Nurses are the wise sages who help you navigate, readjust, and reorient to being thrust by circumstances into the desert of life. They are the one who show you that wells of living water run here too.[24]

Christ, the Blueprint

"In the beginning was the Word, and the Word was with God, and the Word was God. He was with God in the beginning. Through him all things were made; without him nothing was made that has been made. In him was life, and that life was the light of all mankind. The light shines in the darkness, and the darkness has not overcome it."[25]

The Greek word for "Word" that John uses here is *Logos*. One way of understanding what *Logos* means is that it is divine reason. It is the creative force that gives order, form, and meaning. Another way, perhaps more relatable, of saying this is that *Logos* is like a divine blueprint. It gives the layout and the structure; it reveals the purpose, connections, specificities, functions, and it gives meanings to the material. If someone handed you all the components to build a house—wood and nails and shingles and bricks and wires and plumbing—you would probably get a sense of what is intended to be built. But you could just as easily construct an office, go

---

24. See John 4:14.
25. John 1:1–5.

for an open-concept house or one with multiple rooms, you could construct a swanky garage, or even get creative and go for a tree house. Likely, though, you'd end up with "extra pieces" that you wouldn't know what to do with. The blueprint lays out what goes where, how, and for what purpose.

What John is saying is that Jesus is the *Logos* of God: the wise creator that puts all things together as they ought to go. The wisdom behind harmony. The heartbeat of *shalom*. Just listen to someone like Neil deGrasse Tyson talk about how perfect Earth is to sustain life as we know it, and it's not hard to walk away with a deep sense of awe and reverence.

There is a three-tiered wonder of John using the word *Logos*. It means that Christ is the schematics for the cosmos; he reveals to us how we are to be human; and, thirdly, Christ is the perfect revelation of God.

To say it all another way, Christ is the infuser of meaning into all materiality and is the meaning itself. If we want to know how to be human as God is human, and to be human as God intended from the beginning, then we look to Jesus. And, on top of all of that, if we wonder what God is like we look to the blueprint—we look to Jesus. Christ as the *Logos* is a revelation in both directions. To say it yet another way, Christ as the *Logos* is God's blueprint for all of creation and its relationships, and, at the same time, is our blueprint for understanding God. The same way that the definitions of *pneuma* and *ruach* are meant to be conflated, have their definitions interplayed, give nuance, and invite mystery, John's use of *Logos* is meant to do the exact same.

What I find beautiful is that John starts with how the *Logos* is God, then out of that eternal beauty and goodness, that same stuff becomes the blueprint for all of creation. It reveals the naturally outpouring, self-giving nature of God—that the richness and depth of beauty and wisdom that is in God is suffused by God into creation in God's creative act. It's no wonder Richard Rohr, as the good Franciscan he is and taking his cue from Rom 1:20, often says that nature is the first Bible. It gives all the more reason Jesus tells us to "consider the lilies." We might not learn the personal

Christology

name of God, or of God's triune nature, or the church's creeds, or the doxology from nature, but I think we can learn plenty about the nature of God if we did so. The self-expression of the divine is hardly a secret in nature. How stunning that this *Logos*, who is life and in whom all life is held, would imprint on to creation the stuff that also makes for life.

This design of life begetting life is exactly what you get in blood infusions and bone marrow transplants. Creation revealing creator's wisdom and beauty. The wisdom of God who has designed humans to be able to share blood, even to share bone marrow, in order for life to prevail.[26] "In him was life, and that life was the light of all mankind. The light shines in the darkness [of cancer], and the darkness has not overcome it."[27]

Quite literally, the deepest part of ourselves are made to be able to be shared. "But for Adam no suitable helper was found. So the LORD God caused the man to fall into a deep sleep; and while he was sleeping, he took part of the man's side and then closed up the place with flesh. Then the LORD God made a woman from the part he had taken out of the man, and he brought her to the man. The man said, 'This is now bone of my bones and flesh of my flesh.'"[28] Ancient wisdom has known this long before modern medicine ever could. We are created and designed to give and sustain life to one another out of the very stuff we are made of. And we intuitively know that there is nothing deeper to who we are than the marrow of our bone.

When we have a deep intuition or firm conviction we often say we knew it "in our bones." Our language reveals our understanding that whatever happens in our bones is the stuff of life. It is core to who we are. It's only with more modern medicine and technology have we been able to verify this deep knowing—let alone be able to effectively use it to save and sustain another's life.

---

26. Granted, not all blood types are compatible but every type can receive at least its own type as well as O negative.

27. John 1:4–5.

28. Gen 2:20b–23a.

Before bone marrow transplants, patients must go through a "bridging chemo." It is an intense round of chemotherapy with the goal of hopefully wiping out enough that the person would go into remission. During this bridging chemo round we had multiple meetings with oncologists, pharmacists, and the bone marrow transplant coordinator. In these conversations we learned that there is so much more at play in bone marrow transplants than just blood type. Transplant doctors take into account all of the donor's and the recipient's entire HLA typings. Ideally, they are a perfect match, but science has advanced in just the last handful of decades such that they don't necessarily have to be. Successful transplants can come from non-perfect HLA matchings.

The deepest parts of ourselves are made to be able to be shared.

This ever-growing understanding and development in medicine is another aspect of the wisdom of God at work.[29] God is not a clockmaker who set the pieces, kicked off the event, and then stepped back to watch it. God continues to be at work. It is God's grace and wisdom that is incarnated into the hearts and minds of medical professionals. It is God's wisdom that is incarnate in the passions of those who dedicate their lives to cancer research and treatments and cures.

All of this reveals a deep theological truth. Not only is God wise and beautiful in the design of humans to be inherently made to help one another with the very stuff that we ourselves are made of, but this very fact that we are is also a deep affirmation of the faith claim that humanity is made in the image of God.

We too are bearers of life and light. Jesus says, "You are the light of the world,"[30] which, honestly, is a shocking statement from the Word who is life and light himself. We bear what he is. As he said, "Very truly I tell you, whoever believes in me will do the

---

29. The head oncologist at Simon's hospital told us how in his career alone he has seen the success rate of transplants rise from 50 percent to over 90 percent. Praise God! As those familiar with the process know, though, a successful transplant does not necessarily mean survival. The chemotherapies and other treatments wreak havoc on the body.

30. Matt 5:14.

Christology

works I have been doing, and *they will do even greater things than these.*"[31] We have the ability to donate blood and marrow—the essence of our own life—and it can be integrated into the blood and marrow of another, saving their life. "For the life of a creature is in the blood."[32]

We are this way, because God is this way. This is the *Logos*.

During one of those conversations with Dr. Saini during the bridging chemo about what actually happens during a stem cell transplant, all three of us—Mikhaela, Dr. Saini, and myself—ended up in tears. Not because of fear. Not because of the weight of what was to come, as worthy as that would have been. We were all teary because of the beauty. It is good news.

The *logos* that the very stuff of one person can be transplanted into another and engrafted as one's own to save their life is stunningly beautiful. The science and technology and understanding and process is sublime.

It's hard to remember but important nonetheless to keep in mind that chemo is not the enemy: cancer is. Chemo is the hell through which heaven is gained. Chemo is the suffering that produces life. In the hands of the great physician, chemo is the refiner's fire.[33]

We are made in the image of God. And we are also made in the image of each other. Logically, it makes sense—we all share the same starting point, the same blueprint. We are all made in the same image of the same God. This isn't just a metaphysical faith claim. It is a scientific one. We all share a genetic image. Evolutionary biology would tell us the same thing.

Your blood can save my life. Your blood might have saved my son's life. Your donated blood will save someone's life. We share a blueprint. There is a design of what it means to be human that we all share. It's written into our DNA. It is pumped through our veins. It is seen in blood types and HLA typing. It is seen in the willingness to donate blood products. It is seen in our moral

---

31. John 14:12a; emphasis mine.
32. Lev 17:11.
33. See Mal 3:2.

obligations to one another, it's in our kingdom calling to love our neighbor, and it's in the way our cells fit together and sustain life in one another's bodies. We are not our own. Our image is not our own. It is God's image alive in us. And it deeply interlinks us with all other people.

The image within calls us all towards an ethical vision, a moral responsibility.

Kenneth Tanner often says that the goal of humanity is to be human as God is human: "Jesus . . . is the beginning and end of what it means to be human."[34] Which means that to be human as God is human is to be human as Jesus is human. To look to Christ as the blueprint and path forward and model for how we all ought to live. Which, of course, is also what it means to be a disciple or apprentice of Jesus. What Fr. Tanner invokes is that the way of Jesus is the way of full humanity.

Following the way of Jesus is to do as he did. As Jesus said, "Whoever wants to be my disciple must deny themselves and take up their cross daily and follow me."[35] This call to a daily crucifixion is not a metaphor like we too often hear it now. It is a call to be willing to give of ourselves.

Practically and contextually, this looks like donating blood, plasma, platelets, and marrow. This is an enfleshing of the Christ-pattern. Our bodies broken and blood poured out. "But he was pierced for our transgressions . . . and by his wounds we are healed."[36]

To put all of these concepts together: "But if we walk in the light, as he is in the light, we have fellowship with one another, and the blood of Jesus, his Son, purifies us from all sin."[37]

---

34. Tanner, "Made Well."
35. Luke 9:23.
36. Isa 53:5.
37. 1 John 1:7. See also Athanasius, *On the Incarnation*, 52–56. The early church fathers talked about "sin" not just in a moral sense that we are used to today but as a state of corruption. Jesus' saving work, then, is much more like a doctor saving us from cancer than a lawyer saving us from a judgment on our moral wrong, or blame-shifting to a scapegoat.

Christology

If we walk in the light . . . if we live into the image that is within us and beyond us. The image that is within our neighbor. The image that connects and transcends all people. The image that is servant-hearted, that gives of itself for the good of another. The image that is even willing to shed its own blood for the salvation of another.

Is there any truer Christian practice than blood donation?

There is a retired lady at our church who is, in every other respect, anything but retired. I don't know when she ever finds time to rest or to sit down. Even her dreams are probably occupied with how she can help people. I think that Tess might be busier in retirement than she was when she worked and raised her kids.

She is one of the most servant-hearted people I have ever met in my life. She is always using her free time to volunteer, to help, to organize, to clean, to cook for someone else. She opened her house for us to use for our baby shower before Jack was born, and she made almost all of the food for it, too. She gives us exclusive, unlimited pool access so that Simon can avoid the germs of public pools. She regularly volunteers her time at a local assisted living and nursing home, and visiting hospice patients. If she's not there you could find her planting flowers at our church, or mowing the church's grass.

With every church event she jumps at the chance to make thousands of cookies, despite the fact that we don't have much more than a hundred people on a Sunday morning. She preps and makes meals for all of our youth group events, vacuums the church's carpets, deep cleans our children's ministry's toys, runs our coffee and landscaping teams, scrapes bird poop off the front steps, and does anything else she notices might need done. Tess is truly a saint. Of course, she would earnestly deny until kingdom come, which is further proof that it's true.

On top of doing all of that, she is a wife, a mother, and a grandmother, *and* she drives half an hour away to donate platelets every week. Every single week. This might be the only time in her week that she sits still.

Bone of My Bone

She would balk at me making such grand connections, but I truly believe that she is doing the Lord's work: every week Tess presides over the sacrament that is her own body, breaks it, and gives it away so that God will use it to increase life.

Christology

The Cross and Cytarabine

Crucifixion is death;
So is chemo
"therapy"

Death of body—
    death of cells
in the body
    from the body.

Mutate, eradicate
medicate

Blurring the lines
of vitality
and oblivion

In the middle
the cross stands
touching both
    is both.

Hell spits out the Savior
    good news to those imprisoned:
The curse has become the cure.

Glory of Heaven incarnates in Hell.
    Christ alive
    what is this?

Souls alive in the valley of Death.
Christ with us.

I'm asking: is Christ with us?

Cancer is a block to stumble
    and fall
from faith, or
    —just maybe—
into faith.

Upon the cross, piercing his side,

Bone of My Bone

    for good measure
Or
    to place a Broviac—
And
    a port
    "for good measure"

Parched tongue,
raspy words and shedding throat
from the chemical burn,
    the wretched charism

What is reprieve? I hold up to your cracked and peeling lips
a sponge of spoiled tastes, of vinegar wine:
    drink this cup, this Venetoclax

These blurred lines:
The Cross and Cytarabine.

The paradox of Eucharist:
saved through death:
"He will swallow up death forever.
The Sovereign Lord will wipe away
the tears from all faces;
he will remove his people's disease
from all the earth.

The Lord has spoken."[38]
Or so we hope.

---

38. This last stanza borrowed and edited from Isa 25:8.

Salvation

> "Note that the prologue [of John's Gospel] does not say that the Word who existed before creation became a human being (Greek: anthropos), or a man (Gr: aner), but flesh (Gr: sarx), a broader reality."[1]

THE EARLY CHURCH FATHERS had a way of talking about the incarnation of Christ that is also a point about salvation. In my upbringing salvation was a thing that happened when you "invited Jesus into your heart." Typically this just meant praying and confessing that you're a sinner in need of grace. At this point in my life that seems like such a low bar.

Of course I make mistakes. Of course I do harm, sometimes on accident, sometimes on purpose, sometimes carelessly, and sometimes methodically. Salvation understood to be just admitting you've done bad things and need to be forgiven isn't salvation at all. It's a modicum of humility and self-awareness. At risk of saying it too pointedly, most of those sins can be avoided with emotional maturity and healthy relationship skills. God and God's salvation has to be more than just a moral ledger.

What else is wrong with this myopic view of salvation is the theatricality of it. You say some words to ease Grandma's mind, to get the overzealous recent college grad off your back, or because

1. Johnson, *Ask the Beasts*, 195.

you were moved by live music and a charismatic communicator. Sometimes, for extra points with your youth group, you maybe would even do it every retreat or camp trip, soaked in tears, standing from your seat during the altar call, or "making your way down to the front of the stage." (Just me?) And then, boom, it's pretty much done. You go home or back to school or back to your job and you're fired up, floating on that emotional experience, and squeezing the moment for all it's worth for a couple weeks. Then you sin again (and again and again) and wonder if your "salvation" actually took or not. Maybe next year it will.

This is the problem with a phenomenon that many have talked about: it is the problem of sin management. With sin management, the focus is on sin. It's about trying to "sin less." But the eternal life that Jesus offers is more than just what happens when you die. It's more than just a tear-infused prayer at youth group. It's the kind and quality of life here and now that carries on into eternity. It is the future hope becoming a present reality. Even if it comes in shadows and glimpses.

When I was young I never heard anybody talk about salvation as an ongoing process, an ongoing reality that has happened and is happening—a working out of your salvation with fear and trembling.[2] "Salvation"—*sozo* in the Greek—also means "healing," "redeeming," "recovering," "cure," and "restoration."

The biblical and historical view of salvation is so much more wonderful than a moral ledger or a confession of the obvious. The way the early church fathers and mothers would talk about salvation is by saying, "That which is not assumed is not redeemed."[3]

When we talk about salvation, we have to be talking about what God has assumed into God's own self. We have to talk about what God has taken into the divine life. When we talked earlier about solidarity, compassion, and God co-suffering, we were talking about salvation. It is God taking into God's own self in order to bring about something renewed and healed.

---

2. Phil 2:12.
3. Johnson, *Ask the Beasts*, 196.

Salvation

Whatever salvation means, it comes by way of God's assumption into God's own life and story and experience. The question, then, is *what exactly is it that is assumed by Christ in the incarnation*? As our beginning quote says, *sarx* is a broad reality. It is more than just human flesh, or, even more particularly, a man. Elizabeth A. Johnson says, "The flesh assumed in Jesus Christ connects with all humanity, all biological life, all soil, the whole matrix of the material universe down to its very roots."[4] In the assumption of humanity, Christ saves humanity. Even more, in the assumption of creation, Christ saves all of creation. That is the significance of Jesus taking on *sarx* and not just *anthropos*. It is the restoration of all things: *apokatastasis*. "Behold I am making all things new!"[5] God is the one who does a new thing, and makes all things new. Both verb and noun get renewed.

Christ's saving work is not just for human souls. It is for trees and shrubs, grizzly bears and beavers, cockatiels and jellyfish. It is for quarks and atoms and Higgs boson particles. It is for bone cells and blood cells and tissue cells and brain cells and skin cells. God is the one from whom new life flows. As has been said, God is the donated blood, and the stem cells in a transplant.

Salvation is healing, restoration, redemption, wholeness, and cure. And it is for everything.

Chemotherapy is working out salvation with fear and trembling. It is the future hope making its way as a present reality. And, as is true in the blueprint or *logos* of the Christ-pattern, out of death comes life. The hope and prayer of parents and patients and medical practitioners is that the life that comes from all the little deaths beset by chemotherapy is a healed form of life on this side of eternity.

And the hope is rooted in Christ, the one who came, lived, died, and was resurrected. In his assumption of *sarx* he also assumed into the divine life death and Hades. This is how there is divine presence even in the void. The abyss is filled with presence. The groundlessness of childhood cancer is filled with the ground

---

4. Johnson, *Ask the Beasts*, 196.
5. Rev 21:5. See also Isa 43:19–20; Rom 8:21.

of being. When Christ died where else did God go, and what else would we imagine he assumed? In his death, he went to the deepest deaths and brought into that hell the light of all *sarx*.[6] There is hope.

In the resurrection Christ assumed and ushered in the new thing that God is doing and bringing about. He has brought the future here and now. He has given the hope of the future wings in which we can find refuge. "He will cover you with his feathers, and under his wings you will find refuge; his faithfulness will be your shield and rampart."[7] On both sides of the veil, and everywhere in between, there is hope. His faithfulness—the faithfulness of God himself—is our shield and rampart.

"What then was God to do? Or what should be done, except to renew again the 'in the image,' so that through it human beings would be able once again to know him? But how could this have occurred except by the coming of the very image of God, our Savior Jesus Christ?"[8] So Christ comes. He hangs on IV poles. He becomes what we are, that we might become what he is.

Engraftment

"In him we have redemption through his blood."[9]

In the transplant world there is a significant benchmark that indicates a successful transplant called "engraftment." With a bone marrow transplant at least—because that's the only one I'm familiar with—engraftment is a technical designation when the person's absolute neutrophil count (ANC) is 500 or more for three days in a row. Neutrophils are a type of white blood cell and are the standard marker for recovery after chemotherapy treatments. For context, ALL patients might retain an ANC, albeit very low. AML patients—like Simon—and bone marrow recipients are tanked to

6. See John 1:1–5, 14.
7. Ps 91:4.
8. Athanasius, *On the Incarnation*, 63.
9. Eph 1:7.

Salvation

an ANC of zero for extended periods of time. When Simon's ANC would go from zero to something as meager as six after weeks, we would rejoice in the healing—the *sozo*—taking place in his body: "See, I am doing a new thing! Now it springs up; do you not perceive it? I am making a way in the wilderness and streams in the wasteland."[10]

To have an ANC of 500 or more for three days in a row indicates that the donated stem cells have taken residence in the bone and are starting to produce these lovely defensive cells:[11] "My Father will love them, and we will come to them and make our home with them."[12]

We often talk about and think about salvation as a singular event—a one-time moment that happened from which you now live a transformed life. But what the process of engraftment reaffirms is that salvation is an ongoing process.

And salvation often requires much more patience, humility, and surrendering control than we would be comfortable with. Engraftment usually takes two to five weeks after the stem cells were given, which is an eternity in the time warp of the oncology floor. Part of the reason is because when the cells do start to be made again by the new, transplanted stem cells, they are immediately used up. The hellfire that is chemotherapy destroys tissues, especially soft tissues, which results in damage throughout the body including terrible mucositis. Effectively, mucositis is the destruction of the lining of the entire throat and GI tract. It takes weeks to be able to measure new white blood cells because they are busy being used as quickly as they can be made. Salvation and the process of being made new are hardly instantaneous, if they ever are.

As I'm writing this, Simon is six and a half months after the day of his transplant and still has neuropathy in his mouth and

---

10. Isa 43:19.

11. As nice as it would be if this alone was the marker of a successful transplant, there is more that needs to happen. You can be engrafted but not 100 percent donor cells. In fact, it will likely take weeks longer but even then not everyone reaches 100 percent donor cells. Above 96 percent is great.

12. John 14:23b.

can't handle cold things well. As much as he loves the idea of ice cream, he usually only ever eats the toppings or whipped cream. Thankfully, he loves whipped cream with the same fervor other kids love ice cream.

Salvation is a long journey—a lifetime of being saved over and over again. There is no other kind.

Aside from just being a salvation of the body, engraftment is also a great way to understand what Jesus does in the salvation of the soul. By "soul," of course, I mean the entire person. It is the entirety of a person. As Paul wrote, "God made him who had no sin to be sin for us, so that in him we might become the righteousness of God."[13]

He became what we are, that we might become what he is. This is salvation. This is biblical *sozo*. He took on death so that we would have life. He took on corruptibility so that we could take on his incorruptibility.[14] This is the heart of the salvific work of Christ. It is not the image of an angry god, ready to smite someone—or everyone—because somebody's got to pay the price that God set. That conception of God quickly reveals that our true god is some concept of justice that we believe even YHWH is beholden to.

Instead, this divine exchange is the truth of God as God has revealed Godself to be. It is a God who is Father, who is love,[15] who is the physician,[16] who will not stand to see His good, beloved creation fall to sin, death, corruptibility, or cancer. It is a God whose image has imprinted into humanity so that we can give of ourselves for the bodily healing of another, just as he is and has done. The salvific work of Christ is character transformation and growth into Christlikeness to become people like Tess, who make a point to regularly go out of our way and break the bread of our body to donate blood and platelets and plasma. These are the long works of salvation.

---

13. 2 Cor 5:21.

14. 1 Cor 15:53–55. Athanasius' *On the Incarnation* elaborates this beautiful understanding all throughout the book.

15. As 1 John 4 says.

16. Mark 2:17.

Salvation

I know a dear one who passed away who had also received a bone marrow transplant named Emma. We shared a lot of rounds across the hall from each other when we stayed in the hospital with Simon. Those were the days before either one of them received a bone marrow transplant. She unfortunately ended up passing away from complications brought about by the transplant process, but—and I'll never forget—her mom, amidst the lament and grief of the loss of her sweet daughter, also rejoiced that Emma had beaten the cancer. It is a victory that is worth celebrating. Cancer had been defeated. Whether in this life or the next, the cancer is gone. God is still making all things new. Amen and amen.

Engraftment is the same logic that drives Paul's words in Rom 8:15-18 when he declares that we are made into children of God, and thus coheirs with Christ. We see him talk about a grafted body of Christ in Rom 11:11-24. Second Corinthians 5:17 —"Therefore, if anyone is in Christ, the new creation has come: The old has gone, the new is here!"—is language of engraftment, too. Engraftment is a clear and established biblical understanding of God's saving work. People are engrafted in God, by God, for God's good design. It has long been the biblical witness and wisdom. We now just have the medical knowledge and technology to make physical engraftments possible. Whether we are talking about a medical engraftment or a spiritual one, the same truth abides. Engraftment is salvation.

Yet, it is important to stress, engraftment is the initial saving event. To put it in terms of Simon's experience, he engrafted the new stem cells, yet his body faced its toughest challenges even after it was engrafted. It was even after he reached this transplant benchmark that his liver was in major distress and we feared organ failure from veno-occlusive disease. As a result of treating VOD by dehydration, his kidneys were abused and strained, also leading to fears of organ failure in his kidneys. All of this added on to the existent stress from his medicines and chemotherapies being processed by and filtered through his liver and kidneys. These extreme stresses on the organs are unavoidable realities of transplant. There are medical horrors that we now know his oncologist believed he wouldn't survive. Engraftment is a *sozo* event, but as Paul says in 1 Cor 1:18, salvation is an ongoing process: "To us who are being saved..." The cross, like Cytarabine, is foolishness to some but for those who are being saved it is the power of God.

To illustrate the ongoing process and fragility, let's use another image for engraftment.

When my brother and I were young my mom had bought an expensive fruit tree. Part of what made it so exciting was that it was grafted with at least two different kinds of fruit. She was so excited to get this tree and had it planted on the sunny side of the house, which also happened to be the side of the house that had a slight slope to it.

It didn't always snow where we lived outside of St. Louis, and even less often did it snow enough to sled. But it just so happened that the following winter there was enough snow that we thought we would take a sled out. I'm sure you can see where this is going. In our youthful zest for life and joy in the snow, we accidentally plowed over the engrafted tree. We never did get the fruit that the engraftment promised.

Life, faith, and trees are all like that. Just because engraftment happens doesn't mean there won't be major medical concerns still, or young kids with sleds, or life's sufferings. And the concerns are not just whether or not something from outside will infect or affect the body, but fears also fester for what happens internally: Will it take? Will the engraftment stay effective in fighting leukemia? Will the body reject the engraftment, even fight against it? Will the other organs be so badly damaged that my beloved will develop a secondary cancer because of the chemotherapies?

The branch must continue to live and thrive if it will ever produce fruit, which, sometimes—maybe even most of the time—comes with some friction, some suffering. Seeds are not simply born into trees. They must be pressed into the ground. They must break and split open. They start as humble shoots, with roots desperately spreading out to secure the body and absorb nutrients needed for life and growth. The marrow must take residence in the emptied bone. For this to happen, the bone must be stripped

Salvation

of the old marrow, killed by chemicals, and the immune system must be totally annihilated and suppressed, otherwise the donated stem cells would be targeted by the body as a threat. If this rejection happens it's called GvHD: graft-versus-host disease. VOD and GvHD were the two largest concerns our team informed us about before his transplant.

As Simon is now around half a year after he received the stem cells, I can attest that the question of whether the transplant worked or not never quite feels like solid ground. Mostly and assuredly it's the trauma of the experience that won't let me believe it, not fully. Even though he's doing great today. Even though his doctor has even said the words, "The transplant worked." Each clinic visit is exhausting. Not because anything particularly wild is happening but because of the big, bad "What-If?"

I was just getting settled into trusting that Simon had once and for all beaten cancer when we found out he relapsed. To put it lightly, I felt duped. The rug pulled from underneath me, and found myself free-falling into an existential, personal, and faith crisis.

What I find comfort in, however, is the belief that God is still at work. Even on my most agnostic days, I would find comfort in the thought that if there is a God, that God cares and is at work. I don't believe God acted; I believe God is acting—the same God who desires that none should perish but that all experience *sozo*.[17]

To think of salvation as a one-time event is to miss the very heart of God that is always leaning towards restoration, towards fullness, towards liberation, towards healing.

A one-time salvation event also dismisses the very real, always persistent anxiety and fear that comes with cancer, as well as the very real need for a God who is present, who hears the cries of His people,[18] the constant communion of a personal God with God's people. A *sozo* that is a singular event ignores the human condition that we are saved and continually need saving; healed and need healing. Not because we keep messing up and need to be

---

17. See 2 Pet 3:9.
18. Exod 3:7.

rescued from our sin—however true that might be—but because we continue to be human, we continue to live. To be alive is to need *sozo*. It need not always be a moral reckoning.

Salvation, healing, *sozo*, engraftment, or whatever you want to call it cannot be a one-time event. It was, is, and will be. In the eternity of God, *sozo* persists eternally. *Sozo* is the very presence and activity of God. It is the fundamental work of God in the world. For God to exist means *sozo* is an eternal possibility.

We are engrafted and engrafting. Like Simon's little body continues to recover cells, neutrophils and B cells and T cells and platelets, the engraftment continues to work, continues to be a present reality. It is not stuck in the past. It is here and now. Saved and being saved. Salvation has come today to this house![19] And tomorrow we can say the same thing, whatever may come.

This is why the Lord teaches us to pray: "Give us today our daily bread."[20] Tomorrow may I wake up and see that salvation has once again come to this house.

Daily Bread

Salvation often comes as daily bread. Grace enough to just make it through the day.

When Simon relapsed "daily bread" became a mantra, an anchor, a reminder, and a hope. I don't remember the details of when Mikhaela first recited it, just the impact that it had for us. Every day in the day-in-and-out anxieties of his blood counts, praying that the chemo would work to get him into remission, that the stem cells would take, that his body wouldn't reject the donation, that his liver enzymes would come down, that his kidneys could hold on—for this daily bread we would pray. Every day we would come back again and again to that portion of the Lord's Prayer: "Give us this day our daily bread." I don't need to worry about tomorrow,

---

19. Luke 19:9.
20. Matt 6:11.

because I'm worried enough about today. I will seek and ask for daily bread tomorrow, but I need daily bread today.

Daily bread took many forms. Good news was our daily bread. A good nurse was daily bread. A good night's sleep was daily bread. Simon taking a good nap was daily bread. Keith the food service worker was daily bread. Linda and Theresa the housekeepers and their prayers and conversations were daily bread. A good DoorDashed meal was daily bread.

Daily bread is sometimes literal, sometimes not. Sometimes tangible, sometimes not.

Daily bread is whatever is needed to get through the day. It is *manna* in the wilderness. When the Israelites wandered through the desert, God provided them with a bread they'd never had before. A bread they called *manna*—"What is it?"[21] Whatever it was, it was enough. It was enough to get them through the day. Enough to strengthen their bodies to see tomorrow.

Because, O Lord, there are days that are hell. And daily bread is the good news, the small victories, the tiniest things to celebrate, the little interaction or briefest moment of gratitude.

Daily bread is salvation, and salvation is daily bread.

"I Beat It Again"

I was pulling into the Target parking lot, my body riddled with nerves and anxiety. We were all waiting with bated breath for this phone call. I knew the call was coming with some kind of news. I didn't yet know if it would be good or bad, but I did know that I couldn't sit still at home any longer. I couldn't be alone with my Goliath of rampant thoughts and fears. I had to do something normal, something routine. As I was making the turn into the parking lot, Dr. Saini called with the results that Simon had relapsed. I called Mikhaela to tell her. To be honest, the drive home is a blur. I don't remember if I said anything to Simon, who was in the

---

21. Exod 16:31.

backseat unaware of the gravity of the news. I don't remember if I sped home or drove numbly under the speed limit.

I swept up Simon and went into my in-laws' house, and my father-in-law, seeing the agony on my face but not wanting to believe what he inferred, asked what happened. All I could say through my tears was, "It's back. It came back."

That night Mikhaela, Simon, and I got together with her family and had dinner together. Sometimes daily bread is company. Without whom I doubt we would have eaten. We wouldn't have even cared to try.

I sat outside of my body, wedged from myself by grief and terror, as I plucked and prodded a meal I can't remember. "For I eat ashes as my food and mingle my drink with tears."[22] All of us in shock. Ruminating in the disbelief that this would happen again: "he has broken my teeth with gravel; he has trampled me in the dust. I have been deprived of peace; I have forgotten what prosperity is. So I say, 'My splendor is gone and all that I had hoped from the Lord. I remember my affliction and my wandering, the bitterness and the gall. I well remember them, and my soul is downcast within me.'"[23]

During dinner Simon—only just having turned two years old—prophetically roared, "I'll beat it again!" Filled with pride and hope, trusting and believing it to be true more and more each time he said it, we all cried and erupted with cheers and affirmations.

On he went, again and again:

"I'll beat it again!"

"I'll beat it again!"

"I'll beat it again!"

"And a little child shall lead them."[24]

It was the daily bread. More than daily bread, it was loaves and fishes that Christ took and multiplied and fed us with over and over again. We still have not had our fill of what that moment means to us, of those gospel words.

22. Ps 102:9.
23. Lam 3:16–20.
24. Isa 11:6.

And it's not the only moment like that.

During Simon's treatment he spent days in the ICU as a result of the second-worst VOD his oncologist has seen in her career. He was sedated and intubated and had every team in the hospital working on his little body, taking measurements and tests, asking us his baseline behavior and collaborating to make sure our little Simon had the best chances of survival that they could offer.

Because of the sedation he was essentially asleep for days without speaking. We were told that kids often, when they come out of sedation, recall the emotions in the room. They don't remember the words that were shared with them but the impression of how everyone felt. They can recall the feeling that their family thought this was the end of their life, or they recall the feelings of hope, the love and care of the nurses. They remember the love. "By this everyone will know . . . if you love one another."[25] They told us that patting or rubbing or stroking hair doesn't feel good but constant pressure does. When kids are sedated they need to held. They need to be embraced. They need hugged. They need to be spoken to softly, gently, tenderly, and lovingly. Isn't that what we all need?

Simon was sedated and intubated because they feared that his brain was swelling, to which there is no real cure or solution. There's nothing really that can be done to stop a brain from swelling or to reverse the damage swelling causes. Being unconscious calms the brain's activities to not be so active and, hopefully, swell less as a result. And with the stress Simon had on his vital organs, they intubated him proactively in case his lungs or breathing started to give out.

I've never been so desperate to hear my son's voice. It wasn't just the four days he was in the ICU that he didn't speak. He didn't speak for days before that either. The high levels of ammonia in his blood made it so that he was unable to stay awake or really even be cognizant when his eyes were open. Our bubbly boy, full of life and vitality and energy—our boy who would interrupt our adult conversations to say "I want to talk" hadn't spoken a word in over a week.

25. John 13:35.

Lord, how I longed and prayed to hear his voice again. We hadn't heard his voice in so long that we had forgotten what he sounded like. We couldn't remember his real voice. Not his hospital voice. The strained and painful voice. Vocal cords ravaged by chemotherapy and mucositis. We ached to hear his healthy voice. The voice we knew from before. The little raspy textured voice that would say our name to start every conversation, as if there were anyone else around. Would we ever hear it again? Would he recover from this? Will he ever speak again? In an all new way the wisdom of Proverbs rang true: "The tongue has the power of life and death, and those who love it will eat its fruit."[26] We loved its fruit. Craved it.

Then the scans kept coming back with good news. The neurologists were the first to peel off his team. His brain swelling ceased, stopping at minimal swelling, if any, and hopefully without any damage. After forty-eight hours of constant monitors, his brain function had always remained good. His breathing was mostly all on his own, but he stayed intubated "just in case" while he was sedated. But, of course, he was sedated for long enough that they couldn't just stop cold turkey. He would have to be weaned off of the drugs that kept him in limbo.

Those days felt like eternities in themselves. I often half-jokingly say we've already lived three lives. We had our lives before Simon's diagnosis, our lives during his treatments, and our lives after. How often life is marked by major events. We all have our own calendars, don't we? Our souls mark the time. There is a before and an after. Before and after a disease or loss, incarceration or pandemic, marriage or the birth of a child. We all have been shaped by the events of our lives. These events impact and inform how we see, think, spend our time, vote, do or not do something, relate to time, handle our frustrations, and cope with anxiety.

As Simon started to wake up, they told us to not expect him to speak. They would take the intubation tube out but it leaves its own damage on the throat and vocal cords. This damage, of

---

26. Prov 18:21.

course, being on top of the excruciating mucositis damage. Many kids who come off sedation choose not to because of the pain.

Lord, give us our daily bread. I just want to hear my baby's voice again.

There come times where prayers are more like pleas. This was yet another one of those moments. We have had our share and then some of those moments.

Lord, give us our daily bread. Yet, I know, too, that "man does not live on bread alone, but on every word that comes from the mouth of God."[27] And, sometimes, the bread and word of God are one and the same.[28]

Simon opened his swollen little eyes. Just enough. Just enough to see his mommy and say, softly, weakly: "I beat it again."

It would be days still until he would say anything again.

When he did speak again, it was in a rare moment where it was just me and him in the room. Mikhaela had stepped out to eat. Per the bone marrow unit rules, we weren't supposed to eat in the same room as him in case the food carried with it some bacteria or virus. After eating every meal we would have to scrub our hands for two minutes before we entered the room again. I showed him his Avengers ball and pointed to the characters, asking him who each one was. When I pointed to Thor, in a gravely sore voice he responded: "Thor."

He was pained by just one word when a couple days previous he said four: "I beat it again." The salvation of daily bread had come in his having strength to utter four words and again days later with just the one word. Sometimes salvation is like that. It ebbs and flows. But, like tracking blood trends, a day-to-day comparison is less helpful and less informative. Trends over longer periods of time are more useful, more true of the salvific work of God in and through us.

---

27. Matt 4:4 and Deut 8:3.

28. Aside from my following experience, Jesus is attested to being both Word and Bread in John's Gospel. See chapters 1 and 6 of John's Gospel account.

Not every salvation is a lightning flash. Some salvation is more like yeast being worked through dough.[29] Either way it is a moment of transcendence. Something beyond us is happening. It breathes on the fire deep inside, it moves like the *ruach* around us. These are moments where you know the moment is more than what it seems. That moment in the ICU, when he spoke for the first time, was exactly that. It was a revelation: the bread and word were one and the same. The daily bread and the Word were one and the same. And they brought life.

It was Simon's words, but it was more than just his words. It was clarity. It was a type of knowing. As Mikhaela says, it wasn't just God speaking to us through Simon. It was Simon sharing with us from his own relationship with Jesus. He knew. He knew that the work he and God did was enough. And he knew that it was worth pushing through the pain in his throat to tell us.

He was letting us in on the secret: "I beat it again."
He was ministering to our souls: "I beat it again."
He was preaching the good news: "I beat it again."
He was sharing daily bread: "I beat it again."
He was witnessing salvation: "I beat it again."

---

29. Matt 13:13.

Miracles

THIS MAY BE ONE of the more difficult chapters to write. Not because miracles haven't happened, but exactly because they do. They happen all the time and there is no rhyme or reason to them—who receives them and why?

It's not because of some invisible amount of faith or prayer. I know faithful, prayerful people who have lost their children to cancer. To assume we can pray hard enough, believe enough, and God will answer and strike miracles is just a repackaging of the belief that we can control God. As if miracles are like getting a resolution onto a local ballot: if we just get so many signatures that my kid should not die of cancer then God will consider saving them. What a monstrous belief. What a monstrous god.

We cannot control the wind.

I think an entirely different understanding of miracles is needed in general. It isn't whether miracles happen. It's whether we have "eyes to see," as Jesus often said. There's a line from the nineteenth-century poet Elizabeth Barrett Browning that captures it perfectly:

> Earth's crammed with heaven,
> And every common bush afire with God,
> But only he who sees takes off his shoes;
> The rest sit round and pluck blackberries.[1]

---

1. Browning, *Aurora Leigh*.

Is this just a blackberry bush? Are we really here to just pick berries? Or is this sacred ground?

Earth is crammed with heaven. There is a reason that the biblical story begins in a garden. There's a reason the biblical witness is that people are made from the dirt; that God is heard walking through the garden. That leaves and animal skins cover the people's nakedness. There is nowhere else but here. Life is the stuff of God breathed into the stuff of here: "The Spirit of God has made me; the breath of the Almighty gives me life."[2] There is no holier ground than this dirt, than this flesh.

The point isn't that once we die our souls travel somewhere else. The point is that the somewhere else—or, more accurately, the something else—is all in all, here, even in this place. It's why the biblical eschatological vision is that heaven joins Earth.[3] We catch glimpses of this now, but in the restored world we will see fully. Sometimes we can only see blackberry bushes. "For now we see only a reflection as in a mirror; then we shall see face to face. Now I know in part; then I shall know fully, even as I am fully known."[4]

Lord, give us eyes to see that every common bush is afire with you.

When we think about miracles our modern minds get caught up on whether there really was a global flood and a big ark or a burning bush or a split rock. In our debates, we miss the truth while looking for facts.

It is only the one who sees who takes off his shoes, who recognizes the holy is here. The rest are looking at the same bush. They just see it as only a blackberry bush and not what it is: a blackberry bush on fire with God's presence.

It's unhelpful to try and split natural and supernatural. Being products of the "Enlightenment" we are obsessed with "objectivity," as if inescapably subjective humans with subjective vantage points who have been shaped in our subjective formations could

---

2. Job 33:4.

3. Revelation 21 and 22 are prime examples in addition to Jesus' insistent teaching that the Kingdom of Heaven is here, now, and at hand.

4. 1 Cor 13:12.

somehow ever find objectivity and lay claim to it. We overlook the simple reality that Jesus didn't try to split natural and supernatural, nor did the biblical writers.

As the inimitable Jürgen Moltmann has expressed: "Jesus' healings are not supernatural miracles in a natural world. They are the only truly 'natural' things in a world that is unnatural, demonized and wounded."[5] I wonder how much our landscape of Internet personalities that don't match our in-person lives, our constant ego projections on the relationships and situations around us, and our wounded self-image and unnatural hierarchies form us to be people who search, crave, and are satisfied with superficial answers and shallow understandings. We are content being disconnected, demystified, living with dualistic concepts, and artificial relationships—with each other, with God, with creation, and with ourselves.

What I suggest is that in order to witness miracles as such—and to see how widespread they actually are—we need epistemological humility. We need to not believe that we know it all. Enlightenment reasoning is *a way* of understanding, but not *the way* of understanding. In a cold, incarnation-less, reason-is-the-only-truth world, "natural" and "rational" are synonymous, as are "supernatural" and "irrationality."

The problem with this, though, is that the Christian faith is founded upon an irrationality: "We preach Christ crucified: a stumbling block to Jews and foolishness to Gentiles."[6] The mistake is assuming that means it is wrong. Hardly ever do we stop to wonder if our starting point is wrong. Maybe it's not irrational that Christ was crucified and resurrected. Maybe the real irrationality lies in believing a God would be distant, unmoved, un-incarnated. Maybe it's irrational to see a blackberry bush as only just that. I know Christ is alive not because of rationalistic, apologetic arguments for a bodily resurrection, but because I have encountered a living God. I have seen God in the eyes of my children. I have seen

5. Moltmann, *Way of Jesus Christ*, 98–99.
6. 1 Cor 1:23.

new life, and I have seen resurrection. I have seen the world in a grain of sand and heaven in a wildflower.[7]

What is helpful, what is useful, instead of pitting rational against irrational or natural against supernatural, would be to recognize miracles as big and small,[8] yet, still, persistent all the same. Of course, I don't mean to suggest one is better than the other. By "big" and "small" I don't mean to convey a judgment of value. Often the "big" ones are the ones we notice because they are the things we pray for. They are the ones that consume our thoughts the most. But in my experience it's the "small" ones that make the largest difference. Like small degrees of incremental change. We romanticize Saul's encounter on the road to Damascus but overlook the daily practices of formation in our own encounters. The reality is that every journey is one step at a time. When the goal is to hit the moon it becomes a game of thousandths of a degree. These tiny changes in the trajectory will result in either being where we want to be or to miss it by a mile.

In this grace-filled life, in this world that is aflame with divine presence, in this way of seeing that is expectant and anticipatory of God's very self and activity, we can go forward with the assurance that Christ really is all in all. From this place we know that we know that miracles of all sizes abound all the time, because miracles are less about *what* we see and more about *how* we see.

Big Miracles

The Body

In a previous section on *Christ, the Blueprint*, I wrote about the beauty of a bone marrow transplant. Admittedly, saying this sounds like a contradiction of terms. I very much want to keep the

---

7. Blake, "Auguries of Innocence."

8. If we want to categorize them at all! It helps me to think of things in categories as a way of paying attention, but when we talk about God and the things of God all categories should have asterisks to indicate that though we might want to split things neatly, God is always blurring the lines between and moving beyond the categories.

tension, because the tension is reality. The entire process is horrific and also beautiful in its own way. It's terrifying because there's no going around the reality that chemotherapy is, at its basic level, chemicals specifically designed to destroy. It is chemical warfare, pumped directly into the heart. But it's also designed to eliminate the cancerous cells—to wipe them out so the body can express them as waste. The tragic part is that it also wipes out and affects good cells. There is a type of lamentable beauty in the science of it. It is hell and, from the right perspective, it is also bittersweet, because without it the cancer would have killed my son. It is a damnable experience to have to have, *and* it is the only one that treats or cures the disease. The long-term side effects are real, but what else could be expected from a full-scale, warlike chemical assault directed at the smallest of cells? Thus the tension is the reality of it. It is neither all good nor all bad. Being dualistic about it will not be helpful.

But the truest unbridled beauty is the human body. Depleted and drained of life by the ravages of chemotherapy, it recovers again. What else could it mean to speak of the *imago Dei*—the image of God—on an oncology floor except to recognize this Christ-pattern? Out of death comes life. So it is in the life of God; so it is in our inherited image.

The marrow produces neutrophils again, red blood cells, white blood cells, T cells and B cells, and platelets. Ideally, these good, healthy cells recover whereas all the copies of the leukemia have been wiped out, and, what's more, that the body's new transplanted immune system be able to identify and remove them, should they ever crop up again.

The story of Shadrach, Meshach, and Abednego serves as an acute allegory. Refusing to bend the knee to the forces of death, they are thrown into the fire, yet they are not consumed. They come out of the other side because of the one who is in the fire with them.[9]

---

9. Dan 3:16–28.

Bone of My Bone

The Science

Of course, if the body's given immune system isn't capable of identifying malignant cells as such, then it won't be able to fight them off should they ever rear their ugly heads again. In such an instance, as with Simon, more drastic measures are needed. For some it might be CAR T therapy, for others a bone marrow transplant, and for some others both might be needed. It is a miracle that such sciences and technologies exist.[10] To God be the glory.

CAR T-cell therapy is also a medical marvel. Though Simon didn't need this as part of his treatment, we've learned a general idea of it from the nurses and doctors. Essentially, blood is taken from the patient and sent to a lab. In the lab they genetically modify the T cells, reprogramming them to target and eliminate that kid's specific type of cancer. They then take the blood with the reprogrammed T cells and give it back to the child.

A bone marrow transplant is another example of the big miracle that is the human body in partnership with the miracle of science and medicine. A bone marrow transplant means the complete elimination and suppression of the kid's marrow and entire immune system followed by the introduction of a new one through the infusion of stem cells. "Prophesy to these bones and say to them, 'Dry bones, hear the word of the Lord! This is what

---

10. While we rejoice in how far science has gone and taken us, the amount of governmental spending is astronomically low. The National Cancer Institute—the governmental agency responsible for research and education—is allotted $6.4 billion every year (2020). A measly 4 percent of that goes towards all pediatric cancers combined. So many of the standard chemotherapies were created decades ago. Children deserve more than 4 percent. For example, NASA received more than $20 billion from the US government in 2020, the Space Force received around $15 billion (2021), and the US spent $10 billion to build *three* submarines. The moral priorities of a nation are lost when so much is spent on weapons of death and so little on instruments of survival for children.

Miracles

the Sovereign Lord says to these bones: I will make breath[11] enter you, and you will come to life.'"[12]

The beauty of stem cells is that they know where to go, what to do, and what to become. There is a preconscious knowing within the cells themselves. They know to become certain blood cells, and to travel to the empty spaces where marrow once resided. The stem cells are administered in a process that looks just like a normal blood transfusion. They don't have to be injected into the bone. They are hung in a bag and gravity carries it from the IV pole through the tube, through the port or Broviac, and into the heart where it's then pumped around the body and finds its new home.

We see a similar preconscious knowing in other places too. How does a seed know to be a tree and not a flower? How does it know to grow and eventually produce a specific type of seed that catches the wind in a certain way to fly further away so that the new shoots and the parent tree don't have to compete for sunlight and resources? Especially considering the fact that other trees intentionally have heavier and more solid types of seeds—like pinecones and walnuts—that drop down into the shade of the parent tree, yet their competition is not a problem for the seed or parent. So it is with stem cells. They will find the spaciousness in the bones and take residence. From their new home, they will develop into what they need to. They will know to become the stuff of the marrow. "Behold, I am making all things new"[13] includes bone marrows and immune systems. Ancient preconscious knowledge married with sophisticated modern knowledge comes together to create miracles.

"Then the Lord God made a woman from the rib he had taken out of the man, and he brought her to the man. The man said, 'This is now bone of my bones and flesh of my flesh.'"[14] Bone coming from bone, flesh coming from flesh, marrow coming from

---

11. The Hebrew word used here is *ruach*. We could also read it as saying, "I will make Spirit enter you."
12. Ezek 37:4–5.
13. Isa 43:19; Rev 21:5.
14. Gen 2:22–23a.

marrow. This design of the human body has been an ingrained miracle since the beginning that science only now is recognizing.

Simon's blood type is changed from his original O+ to A+, but he will always have both phenotypes. To borrow a Christological term: his own body has become a hypostatic union. Two are inseparably one. Two phenotypes—his original still found in his saliva and his new one found in his blood. The original phenotype with his original DNA, uniquely given to him by the original combination of mine and Mikhaela's own DNA, which we ourselves inherited as a unique mixture of our parents' respective DNA. Bone of our bone. But his blood will be that of the little girl, given to her by her parents. Blood of their blood. This humbling fact is the reminder that we do not belong to ourselves: we all belong to each other. Science has caught up with what has been true all along.

Like I've said, I do not know the little girl or her parents, and I never will. But, to me, they are his aunty and uncle. They are, in quite a literal way, his godparents.

I will always love them. But I will never meet them. I won't get the opportunity to meet them. I will never see them on this side of eternity. Even if I did, I wouldn't know who they were. Maybe I already have crossed paths with them. Maybe we shop at the same grocery store. Maybe the dad was the bank teller who deposited my money or helped me get a car loan. Maybe the mom was the woman working the booth at the city farmers market. Maybe we sat across the aisle from each other on a flight or sat next to each other on a beach vacation.

And I think maybe that's kind of the point. I find something beautiful about the mystical belief that any given stranger could be Simon's godparents. If Christ is in every stranger, then Simon's donor and his godparents can be every stranger I encounter. With that, somehow, I'm sure you are reading this. Thank you. Thank you for what you did.

Miracles

Rejoicing in Singing[15]

That same day that Simon first roared "I beat it again!" was the day of another miracle. We were at Mikhaela's parents' house with the family. Off in the other room, Simon was playing by himself. The adults were lamenting—itself a holy act—together in the dining room. All of a sudden our attentions were enraptured by a sweet, small voice rising from that other room. We could hear Simon singing the chorus of "Jireh" by Elevation Worship and Maverick City Music. He was singing about God's provision, God's protection, and about how God is always and forever enough for whatever situation we face in life. A prophetic word, without a doubt.

We hadn't been listening to that song. Nobody had mentioned it. The Holy Spirit was moving in Simon, speaking to his little heart, steeling his soul for the long, difficult journey ahead, and through him doing the same for all of us, too. I've always been skeptical of speaking in tongues but now I understand it sounds like a two-year-old singing in the other room.

There is no way to explain this other than to recognize it for what it is. A miracle, an encounter of the divine within the ordinary. A song becomes more than just a song. A word becomes the Word. The holy has appeared in the fervor of a child's singing.

Have you ever had this experience before? This experience where the ordinary becomes saturated with the divine? Or, what's more true, is that we see that this was never just a blackberry bush.

Small Miracles

DoorDash was our crutch and comfort while we lived in the hospital with him. Food was the one thing we could control, and the one thing we had to look forward to every day. We've always been foodie kinds of people. No disrespect to anyone else, but the "food-is-just-sustenance" perspective is completely foreign to us. Cooking, eating, sharing a meal—to me, these are the pinnacle of mundane-yet-sacred moments.

15. See Zeph 3:17.

Bone of My Bone

The conversion of Zacchaeus was at his home, presumably over a meal. The just-resurrected Christ appeared to his disciples on the beach and the first thing he did was invite them to share a meal with him. The Bible is full of imagery of meal-sharing and banquets and feasts. Jesus even taught about the life to come and the fully realized kingdom by talking about feasts.

Before his transplant Simon was an adventurous eater. He tried foods that we were trying for the first time too. He was less than a year old when he tried Afghani food. I was almost thirty. He feasted on falafel, katsu, samosas, paneer tikka masala, drunken noodle, lamb, and kebabs regularly. Being at a hospital in a major city has its upsides in the DoorDash department.

Yet, despite his adolescent willingness to try so many new foods, he has never gone for sandwiches. The only sandwich he will go for is an Uncrustable. Even as I'm writing this he still won't eat a normal, homemade PB&J. He won't eat a cheeseburger or chicken sandwich. He won't eat a deli sandwich either. He doesn't even touch it. He gags at the thought of eating deli meats. But he will demolish hummus like nobody's business.

Then we went into BMT and his taste buds changed. In the process of the chemotherapy destroying the soft tissues in his mouth and GI tract this means it also ruins flavors and the ability to taste. Some kids crave sauces so they can get a semblance of flavor. Some kids need bland foods because the chemo and medicines make them feel sick. Some kids find that they crave spicy food. For a couple days Simon was very into Cool Ranch Doritos until he ate so many he got sick on them, but that will ruin a food for pretty much anyone. But five days before being admitted to the transplant unit he started to eat sandwiches. Of course, it was short-lived since in less than a week from that point he was inundated with chemo and medicines. Now he's back to Uncrustables being the only sandwich he will eat.

We could see that as normal development for a child. But "normal" is not a thing to take lightly on an oncology floor. "Normal" *is* a miracle. It is daily bread. It may be small and ordinary, but that doesn't make it any less miraculous. Whenever a kid can

Miracles

be a kid, in whatever way that comes, it is a miracle. As parents, it's heartbreaking to see your kid unable to do the things they want to do, the things they should be doing as kids. "Normal" is "common grace," as John Wesley would call it. It is grace that is widespread and common to all. "Normal" is a bush on fire with God's presence. Yet "normal" to most is just plucking blackberries. Do we have eyes to see that even picking blackberries is miraculous?

I remember the feeling of dread associated with lamenting the loss of "normal." I remember crying and praying and pleading with God for "normal." How desperately I just wanted to be home, annoyed at my kid because he wasn't listening. How desperately I wanted to be inconvenienced by changing so many diapers in a day and that being the biggest concern. "Normal" is a gift. It is the grace of God. As Jesus said, "God causes his sun to rise on the evil and the good, and sends rain on the righteous and the unrighteous."[16]

The sun is God's. It is neither impersonal nor ours to claim and keep. The sun and rain are daily provisions. They are not cogs of an impersonal, cosmic, clockwork-type system. They are the miracles that God calls forth each day.

God's grace is not an interruption to the normal activity of the day. It is the fabric of our daily life. It is the collapsing of the natural and supernatural. It is the refusal to bifurcate reality. It is recognizing that these are the same reality: the mundane is the sacred. Eating a sandwich is holy. Normalcy is divine.

When "normal" is threatened and the plans we thought were laid out for us are dashed, we can see "normal" for the blessing that it is. In the cracks of our plans we can see divinity. Jeremiah's record of the Lord's words land differently: "'For I know the plans I have for you,' declares the LORD, 'plans to prosper you and not to harm you, plans to give you hope and a future.'"[17]

The Lord's words through Jeremiah become much less rote. Less bumper-sticker, feel-good theology. They become salvific

---

16. Matt 5:45.
17. Jer 29:11.

hope, a light bursting through the fissures of our best-laid plans. They become the hope of a "normal" life.

They become, too, hope in the way of Camus' rebel. Facing the existential threat of cancer and all that comes with it, they become a grounding reminder that no matter what happens, Jesus is on the other side of this. God's words through Jeremiah become the shout into the void, the pushback against the two greatest threats to humanity: despair and death.

And the daily practice of embodying this hope is to eat Afghani food. It means to live into the proleptic hope of "normal" here and now, despite circumstances. It is to find new "normals," new routines. To live into the reality of Jeremiah's words is to celebrate when your child eats a sandwich. It is to consider the birds of the air[18] and the lilies of the field.[19] It is to live deeply embodied and incarnational. It is noticing the miracle of the "normal."

Miracles do not happen in the abstract. They are material. They are bread and fish, sun and rain, sandwiches and tikka masala. It is no ordinary blackberry bush. It is the dwelling place of God. Like Pope Francis wrote: "Nothing in this world is indifferent to us."[20]

Nothing is indifferent to us because it all bears the presence of a God who is also not indifferent to us.

Thank God for all of it. Thank you, God, for each overlooked provision. For nurses and doctors who have become like family. For life-saving medicines. For science. For people who follow their passions. For OTs and PTs and nutritionists and music therapists. For supportive families and friends who met us in the parking lot just to listen. For breakfast burritos and custodians. For daily bread. For hope. For the gift of sleep. For all of these provisions we give thanks to God our provider: Jehovah Jireh.

---

18. Matt 6:26.
19. Luke 12:27.
20. Francis, *Laudato si'*.

Miracles

Splinters

"Cast all your anxiety on him because he cares for you."[21]

Do you know that feeling when something happens and you think, *Why on earth did I do that?* A few days before Simon's scheduled admission for his bone marrow transplant he had a last hurrah before isolation with his buddy Isaac, who is about the same age. Mikhaela took Simon and met up with Isaac and Isaac's mom Brittany, who is one of our dearest friends, so that all four of them could go on a walk together on the bike trails by our house. On these trails there is a bridge that goes over a creek, guarded on either side by wood rails.

As a family we've walked this path countless times, crossed this bridge more times than we could count, and we regularly lean against the wood railings to peer down and watch the water of the creek far down below. Of course this time would be different. Simon, in his excitement from being on a walk with his friend, ran his hand across the railing, drew his hand back and had gotten five splinters. Mikhaela and Brittany, who is a nurse, were able to get most of them out but a couple broke off and were stuck deep down in his skin.

A few days later and it was the day before admission to the bone marrow unit, and Simon had an appointment with his oncologist. We told Dr. Saini about the splinters, being that they are an infection risk for anybody. Most people have a healthy enough immune system to be able to fight off any bacteria from a splinter, but we knew his immune system had already taken a heavy hit from the bridging chemo before transplant. That, and we knew that in a few days he would become entirely defenseless to every little germ.[22] A simple splinter became a potential life-threatening infection risk.

---

21. 1 Pet 5:7.

22. For reference, even after he was engrafted, salt and pepper posed a threat if they were added after the food was already cooked.

Mikhaela felt terrible, racked with guilt and shame. We tried to talk it out, to talk about how it's just a freak accident, to talk about how there was no way to know and that she shouldn't beat herself up over it. But she bore the weight of feeling responsible for him getting splinters, and we both felt the weight of the impending transplant and terrifying potentials that an infection could cause.

Unless you've been in a similar situation, it's hard to imagine just how much everything feels like a threat. A kid next to you in line at the grocery store with a runny nose is never just because of allergies. You can't risk it. Sniffles are always a big deal. Simon coughing just to clear his throat signaled to our central nervous systems a life-threatening danger. Even after Simon was engrafted, recovered, and was well enough to go home he couldn't go outside if the neighbors were cutting their grass because it kicks up too many mold spores into the air.

With an experience like BMT—the lead-up, during, and after—your central nervous system is in a constant state of extreme stress and anxiety. The most primitive and basic part of your brain is firing nonstop in a way that causes you to perceive everything as a threat.[23] Even tiny splinters can keep you up at night and deepen the sinking pit in your stomach. Terrified of the threat posed by tiny splinters in Simon's hand, we spent the rest of the day and night praying.

The next morning we woke up from our too-little sleep early, full of fear, because it was the day we moved into the bone marrow unit. We went in as the three of us, and were terrified of the very real possibility that we might leave just the two of us. We were fearful of the chemo. Fearful of the mucositis. Fearful from all of the side effects listed in the one-and-a-half-inch thick binder they gave us to read. Fearful for his organs. Fearful of the splinters.

What we didn't recognize when we woke up that day was that, however full of fear the day was, it too was the day of the Lord: "For you know very well that the day of the Lord will come like a thief in the night."[24] Coming swiftly, discreetly, powerfully as

23. Tippett, "1,129: Christine Runyan," 4:31–5:14.
24. 1 Thess 5:2.

Miracles

we slept, God was at work. A divine saboteur against the forces of death. In the morning we woke up to the miracle of disappearing splinters. The splinters were gone. Even the deepest shard of wood had simply vanished.

Splinters coming out is a small miracle in any other circumstance. It probably even sounds a little absurd to call it a miracle. Even if we do call it a miracle by any respect it is certainly a small one: surely the creator of everything can remove a couple splinters. God isn't just the God of the big things. Jesus multiplying bread and fish and God releasing Peter from prison are not any more of a miracle than disappearing splinters.

We learned that morning that every day is the day of the Lord. "Because of the Lord's great love we are not consumed, for his compassions never fail. They are new every morning; great is your faithfulness."[25] Another reminder of daily bread. "This is the day that the Lord has made; let us rejoice and be glad in it."[26] Not just the big days, the important days, the days that change the course of human history, but the days that could change our histories; the days that change the course of our lives. Even too, the days that we live and forget.

What a grace it is to have days that we live and forget.

Each day, as we live it, deserves recognition as a gift. Every moment, every breath, a miracle. The things we are concerned about and the things that we don't even know to be concerned about. None of them are too big or too small to be beyond the sight and love of God.

No cancer diagnosis or splinter is too big or too little.

The presence and the activity of God are the normal stuff of life. It is a wonderful thing when we choose to trust that the ins and outs, from the biggest details and severest implications down to the smallest, are all in the loving hands of a loving God.

---

25. Lam 3:22–23.
26. Ps 118:24 NRSVue.

Prayer

We have known the staff at Simon's hospital for over two years now. And we know that they are all more than a little superstitious.

When kids are planned to be released at the end of their chemotherapy round nobody will say that they are going home. It's taboo. As if saying "home," or "*the H word*," as they say, will jinx it. Instead, kids are "going to the zoo."

I've also never seen so many people knock on wood or do it so often.

This superstitious practice at first felt especially ironic at this hospital. This bastion of medical intellect and education. A nationally recognized and awarded site of erudition, and, at the end of the day, they are all still knocking on wood.

This could seem to some as a lack of faith, but, it's actually an immense amount of a type of faith. It is the full recognition that things are out of ultimate control. Where control ends is exactly where faith begins. Few know that crossover better than those who work in oncology.

Just because a chemo road map worked for one kid does not mean it will work for the next, and nobody can explain why. A fever can pop up at any time and extend the inpatient stay. Kids can go into remission after one round of chemo or can battle their disease for years. As smart, skilled, and knowledgeable as they are, there is always more beyond reach. Science is not so different from theology after all.

Prayer

One day, when Simon had a visit at the outpatient clinic, Mikhaela and I were talking with Dr. Saini and somehow we started talking about how widespread the wood-knocking superstition is around the hospital. We told her how we have never seen so many people knock on wood, or be so compelled to do it ourselves. In this moment of self-reflective awareness we were all laughing about it when it hit me: in reality it's actually not so different from prayer. In fact, it's not different at all. Ultimately, the heart of it is the same. It is an ask for help, for goodness, for things that are beyond one's own power to be taken care of.

It radically altered my understanding of what was happening. Seconds before I was laughing about this new compulsive habit I picked up, feeling self-aware and playfully insecure. In a flash these feelings transformed into a type of reverence. I could see all of the times Dr. Saini or the nurses or the music therapist or Mikhaela or myself knocked on wood, and I understood that it wasn't just some lame attempt at control, or a kind of generic well-wishing sent into a void like flipping a coin into a fountain. It was prayer by another name, but it was still prayer. The longing for goodness, for help, for wisdom, for peace. It was the same impulse.

At the end of the day, what's the real difference between knocking on wood and making the sign of the cross?

Our doctors and nurses are not superstitious. They are prayerful. Their contextual way to pray is to knock on wood. It was a revelation of the tenderness, of the humanity, of the love that these doctors and nurses hold for their patients. They do not knock on wood to ward off a jinx. They knock to say *"amen"* to their unspoken prayers. They knock to say, *"Let it be so."* They knock to say, *"Lord, help us."*[1] They knock to say, *"Lord, I believe; help my unbelief."*[2]

---

1. Which is what the biblical word *hosanna* means, even though we use it and typically only think of it as a praise.
2. See Mark 9:24.

What Is Prayer?

"But when you pray, go into your room, close the door and pray to your Father, who is unseen. Then your Father, who sees what is done in secret, will reward you."[3]

Everything is a prayer on an oncology floor.

And I don't mean this in a dramatic or contrived way to prove a point. Prayer is not just clasped hands and heads bowed. I don't think you have to have a special room in your house. That's not what Jesus was getting at. As Paul instructed, "Pray without ceasing."[4] We can't be expected to hole up in a room in our house for our entire lives.

What Jesus is saying about prayer isn't about the mechanics of what your body is or isn't doing, but about the intention, your will. That's why he says, "And when you pray, do not be like the hypocrites, for they love to pray standing in the synagogues and on the street corners to be seen by others. Truly I tell you, they have received their reward in full."[5]

They have already received their reward. The thing they really want is to be noticed, to be thought of as a prayerful person. They want some kind of notoriety or social standing for praying in public. You don't stand on a street corner praying unless you want to be seen.

Of course you *are* able to pray without ceasing *and* leave your house. That is, there is a way that you can pray on street corners and nobody even knows you're praying. Because the prayer, though it might be for the people around you, isn't centered on them seeing you doing it. That isn't the purpose of prayer: to be seen as a prayerful person.

The purpose of prayer is so much deeper than that. The purpose of prayer—whether through intercession, petition,

---

3. Matt 6:6.
4. 1 Thess 5:17.
5. Matt 6:5.

Prayer

thanksgiving, or contemplation—ultimately is about communion with God.

Most prayers in my experience are asking God to change a situation. Oncology prayers often take this shape. "Take away the cancer." "Let her sleep well tonight." "Please, God, let the test come back benign." "Help me with the bills piling up."

I don't want to give the impression that enough prayer or enough faith will cure cancer. I don't think God is waiting for a quota to be met in order to act. That would be a monstrous god and not at all the loving Abba revealed by Jesus, and certainly not worthy of adoration. Yet, still, we wrestle with the tension of stories like Josh 10:12-13 where he prays and the sun and moon stood still and the daylight was prolonged "about a full day." We wrestle with stories today about God answering prayers in powerfully clear ways, while also not wanting to contribute to any harmful ideologies that we can control God with enough faith or prayers. Jesus doesn't say the poor in spirit will, someday, have the kingdom of heaven. He says it is theirs now. The spiritually bankrupt possess the full kingdom already. Rest, my weary friends. You do not need to pray harder or have more faith in order to move God. God is not distant, nor is God slothful, nor is God uncaring, nor is God a sleeping giant that needs a loud racket to be woken up. God cannot be controlled, and need not be convinced. God is already on your side.[6]

With all of this being said, I do think God changes situations. Maybe not always as dramatically as we would like, though sometimes. In the same way as with miracles, I think God is always at work if even God's actions and movements are subtle shifts so

---

6. I can imagine the next line of questioning, because it's also my own: If God is loving and good and powerful and on my side then why this diagnosis or loss or suffering? To be clear, I don't know why evil and suffering happen, and I don't think we ever will. I think some theological explorations into it are more stomach-able than others. I'll share that what has been happening in my own mind is a dissatisfaction with the classical Christian understandings with more of a curious openness towards Open and Relational and Process thoughts on the matter. Regardless, I am more interested not in the "why" but in the "What now?" given that evil and suffering do happen.

smooth that they could be imperceptible if we're not paying deep attention. Prayer is the act of paying attention.

There is a giving and a receiving in prayer. There is an ask or a question and a listening. Prayer is a conversation, not a monologue. We must speak and we must listen. More often than not I think the more important of the two is to listen. I think if we listen we might get the answers to our questions before we ever even ask them. Maybe even before we have the right words to formulate the question, because God is always at work, always on the move, always working for good. We can even come to find in this that God is the one who is praying in us.[7] Imagine that: God resides within you, praying and interceding to the God who surrounds you, for the work and power of God to abide with you. We are situated to find rest amidst the presence and work of God swirling around us: "Deep calls to deep in the roar of your waterfalls; all your waves and breakers have swept over me."[8]

In so many ways, this entire writing project feels like that for me. I have struggled for a long time wondering where God is. There were days in the hospital where I wondered if God existed at all. Most days I believed there was a God, but I doubted whether God could be trusted. This book feels like a reflection on where God is on an oncology floor and in the midst of pediatric cancer, and, as I am writing, God's presence, love, and action become clearer and clearer.

Everything is a prayer on an oncology floor, because you live in a constant state of needing connection with a loving presence, with hope, with peace and power. Your soul is stripped bare and always open. Hoping, listening to wherever there might be good news.

Everything takes a prayerful posture when everything is on the line.

---

7. Rom 8:26–27.
8. Ps 42:7.

Prayer

Show Me Where It Hurts

We can't overlook Jesus' revolutionary revelation of God as "*Our Father.*"[9] This is a key understanding of how God changes situations. It is the efficacy of prayer, if we dare use such a cold, transactional word.

Simon is as rambunctious as any other almost-three-year-old. He loves to jump on the couch and to jump on us. He runs around turns without much concern for corners of coffee tables or kitchen islands. He has climbing blocks that he loves to climb up and jump off from. What I'm trying to say is that he gets his fair share of bumps and bruises.

When he "bonks" he'll tell us, "Mommy, Daddy, I bonked my head. Will you kiss it?" We know, as does he, that kissing it doesn't heal anything. I don't have medicine in my lips. Kissing a boo-boo doesn't reduce swelling or bruising or stop bleeding.

But it does make a difference.

It often slows down tears. It allows him to take deeper breaths. Being held calms his central nervous system out of its fight, flight, or freeze response.[10] Sometimes when Simon gets hurt, he just yells "No!" at the pain until it goes away. It is prophetic and hilarious all at once.

These changes brought about by kissing bumps and bruises are subtle changes. Imperceptible, even, if we don't know what to look for. Yet, our kisses do make a real change. It might not stop the sun from setting like Joshua's prayer, but in those moments Simon seeks and finds comfort: "Ask and it will be given to you; seek and you will find; knock and the door will be opened to you."[11] That is what a good father does, what a good parent does. To say that bringing emotional comfort is not making a change is to

---

9. It's notable that when asked how to pray, these two crucial words are how he begins: a communal and intimate relationship with the Creator.

10. Tippett, "1,129: Christine Runyan," 14:43–17:34.

11. Matt 7:7.

undervalue the human psyche, spirit, and soul in favor of a purely mechanical view of the body.[12]

There seems an implicit understanding by Simon that our kisses won't take the pain away, but that they offer something else. They communicate love and belonging. It instills the deep truth that "I might be injured but I am still loved."

Such is the truth of boo-boos, and it is the truth of a cancer diagnosis. I might be injured but I am still loved. And it is the truth of prayer. Amidst our pain, our grief, our confusion, our spiritual crises, and our diagnosis God is inviting us: "Show me where it hurts."

Prayer is our response to that invitation. It doesn't have to be scripted or eloquent, and it doesn't even have to be nice. It can be full of profanity and tears and silence and rage. There are even times where it should be. Because then it's honest. Then we're really showing God where it hurts and why and how badly.

God responds and even *pre*sponds, should we have the hindsight to see it, working in subtle ways like a kiss on a "bonk."[13] The wound may throb, the bruise may spread. But we are comforted by our Father. We are loved. I might be injured but I am still loved.

What a powerful proclamation we could make over our lives! How might our trauma begin to be healed if we took up that mantra? *I might be injured but I am still loved.* We do not have to pretend the pain is not there. We do not have to rush healing. We can recognize that we are still injured *and* we are still loved. One does not mean the other can't also be true.

How might we begin to heal the narratives we hold to be true? Just a couple weeks ago Simon took a nap that was over two

---

12. My dear friend Matt, who is a nurse practitioner working in hospice, has helped me see how traditional medicine in America too often makes this trade, and then leads us to believe that the body is the only concern or metric for the "health" of the person with almost total disregard to these other facets of what it is to be human. From a theological perspective, Dr. Randy Woodley talks often against the bifurcation of our understanding of a human person into a reductionistic dualism (*Indigenous Theology*, 63).

13. At this point I hope the notion has become clear that "subtle-yet-changed" is the speed of God.

Prayer

and a half hours long. Where most parents would rejoice, I was terrified. I was terrified that something must be wrong. He must be sick. The cancer must be back. How easy it is for trauma to inform our narratives, since trauma changes the wiring of our brains. I had to interrupt my internal spiral and tell Mikhaela of this fear I was harboring. We paused on our way out the front door and she reminded me of what we knew to be true that day. He is growing. He is good. His counts were great from his last visit.

I might be injured but I am still loved.

Prayer is this conversation. Prayer is God asking us where it hurts and us showing God our wounds. Prayer is receiving God's comfort at the site of our injuries. There is something inexplicably wholesome and beautiful about leaning into comfort and remembering that we are loved. In this flow of prayer we come to experience that prayer is communion with God. It is connection and kinship. It is resting in the one whose image we are created in.

Prayer is like breathing. It is taken in, given out, taken in, and given back out again. Prayer on an oncology floor is God asking us where it hurts, letting out the truth of our pain, receiving comfort and communion, and putting back out that same comfort for others. Like Fr. Richard Rohr has written, "If only we could see these 'wounds' as *the way through*, as Jesus did, then they would become sacred wounds rather than scars to deny, disguise, or project onto others."[14]

Sometimes it might be for others in similar situations. So many organizations and foundations are started by bereaved parents to lend comfort, aid, and assistance to families going through similar experiences as they went through.

Or it might be in your general attitude towards others. It can be an experience that cracks open our pride and ego and lets us be softer towards one another. Mikhaela is one such soul. She lives out Fr. Rohr's words well: "If we do not transform our pain, we will most assuredly transmit it."[15] She tries unbelievably hard to

---

14. Center for Action and Contemplation, "Transforming Pain" (emphasis original).

15. Center for Action and Contemplation, "Transforming Pain."

transform her pain. Or, more accurately, to allow God to transform it. Like taking bread, lifting it up, and giving thanks: we trust that God will make it into a Eucharist. She does this with her own experiences.

As such, prayer is also the avenue through which *we* are changed. Through prayer we become transformed and transfigured. The more we can do this breath-like prayer process—inhale and exhale, in and out, receive and give—then the more we will be changed. We are able to take the alchemy of that holy work and offer it as our own Eucharist. Brian McLaren wrote, "The authentic experience of communion with God leads into communion with all God's creations. The deeper we go into the love of God, the deeper we are led into all that God loves."[16]

Ultimately, then, above all, we could say prayer is the avenue *par excellence* through which we commune with God and are changed by God. It is no wonder why Jesus would often go off to be alone to pray. Nor is it a surprise that one of the most theologically profound moments in the Gospels—when Jesus submits and unites the human will to the divine will at Gethsemane—is during a time of prayer.

We do not have to cross our fingers or knock on wood to ward off bad vibes or jinxes. Our knocks instead can be an "amen." God knows and sees and cares and loves and will work and move, because God has always known and seen and cared and loved and worked and moved. Through prayer may we have eyes to see. Amen.

---

16. McLaren, *Faith After Doubt*, 182.

Eschatology

"Therefore I tell you, do not worry about your life, what you will eat or drink; or about your body, what you will wear. Is not life more than food, and the body more than clothes? Look at the birds of the air; they do not sow or reap or store away in barns, and yet your heavenly Father feeds them. Are you not much more valuable than they? Can any one of you by worrying add a single hour to your life?
"And why do you worry about clothes? See how the flowers of the field grow. They do not labor or spin. Yet I tell you that not even Solomon in all his splendor was dressed like one of these. If that is how God clothes the grass of the field, which is here today and tomorrow is thrown into the fire, will he not much more clothe you—you of little faith? So do not worry, saying, 'What shall we eat?' or 'What shall we drink?' or 'What shall we wear?' For the pagans run after all these things, and your heavenly Father knows that you need them. But seek first his kingdom and his righteousness, and all these things will be given to you as well. Therefore do not worry about tomorrow, for tomorrow will worry about itself. Each day has enough trouble of its own."[1]

---

1. Matt 6:25–34.

Bibliography

Athanasius. *On the Incarnation.* Translated by John Behr. Yonkers, NY: St. Vladimir's Seminary Press, 2011.
Balthasar, Hans Urs von. *Love Alone Is Credible.* Translated by D.C. Schindler. San Fransisco: Ignatius, 2024.
Blake, William. "Auguries of Innocence." Public Domain Poetry. https://www.public-domain-poetry.com/william-blake/auguries-of-innocence-9210.
Bonaventure. *The Soul's Journey into God.* Translated by Ewert Cousins. Mahwah, NJ: Paulist, 1978.
Brown, Brené. "Listening to Shame." TED, March 2012. Video, 18:46–19:10. https://www.ted.com/talks/brene_brown_listening_to_shame/transcript.
———. "The Power of Vulnerability." TED, June 2010. Video, 15:36–16:38. https://www.ted.com/talks/brene_brown_the_power_of_vulnerability/transcript.
Browning, Elizabeth Barrett. *Aurora Leigh.* Ebook. London: Bradbury and Evans, 1857. https://www.gutenberg.org/cache/epub/56621/pg56621-images.html.
Burton, Neel. "The Difference Between Empathy and Sympathy." Psychology Today, June 24, 2024. https://www.psychologytoday.com/us/blog/hide-and-seek/201505/the-difference-between-empathy-and-sympathy.
Center for Action and Contemplation. "The Scandal of the Particular and the Honor/Shame System." June 24, 2015. https://cac.org/daily-meditations/the-scandal-of-the-particular-and-the-honor-shame-system-2015-06-24/.
———. "Transforming Pain." October 17, 2018. https://cac.org/daily-meditations/transforming-pain-2018-10-17/.
Comer, John Mark. *Practicing the Way: Be with Jesus. Become Like Him. Do as He Did.* New York: Waterbrook, 2024.
Cone, James. *Black Theology & Black Power.* Maryknoll, NY: Orbis, 1997.
Delio, Ilia. *The Emergent Christ: Exploring the Meaning of Catholic in an Evolutionary Universe.* Maryknoll, NY: Orbis, 2011.
Enns, Pete. "Episode 29: Grace Ji-Sun Kim—A Theology of Visibility." In *Faith for Normal People Podcast.* November 13, 2023. Podcast, MP3 audio,

Bibliography

11:47–12:00. https://thebiblefornormalpeople.com/episode-29-grace-ji-sun-kim-a-theology-of-visibility/.

Francis. *Laudato si'*. Vatican, May 24, 2015. https://www.vatican.va/content/francesco/en/encyclicals/documents/papa-francesco_20150524_enciclica-laudato-si.html.

Greer, Broderick. "Mary's Rebel Anthem." On Being, January 30, 2017. https://onbeing.org/blog/broderick-greer-marys-rebel-anthem/.

Irenaeus. *On the Apostolic Preaching*. Translated by John Behr. Yonkers, NY: St. Vladimir's Seminary Press, 1997.

Jennings, Willie James. *Acts*. Louisville: Westminster John Knox, 2017.

Jersak, Bradley. *Her Gates Will Never Be Shut: Hell, Hope, and the New Jerusalem*. Eugene, OR: Wipf & Stock, 2009.

Johnson, Elizabeth A. *Ask the Beasts: Darwin and the God of Love*. London: Bloomsbury, 2014.

Julian. *Revelations of Divine Love*. Translated and edited by Barry Windeatt. Oxford: Oxford University Press, 2016.

Kärkkäinen, Veli-Matti. *Pneumatology: The Holy Spirit in Ecumenical, International, and Contextual Perspective*. Grand Rapids: Baker Academic, 2002.

Koyama, Kosuke. *Water Buffalo Theology*. London: SCM, 1974.

Lewis, C. S. *Till We Have Faces: A Myth Retold*. Kindle. San Fransisco: HarperOne, 2017.

McLaren, Brian. *Faith After Doubt: Why Your Beliefs Stopped Working and What to Do About It*. St. Martin's, 2021.

Merton, Thomas. *The Wisdom of the Desert*. New York: New Directions, 1970.

Migliore, Dan. *Faith Seeking Understanding: An Introduction to Christian Theology*. Grand Rapids: Eerdmans, 2014.

Moltmann, Jürgen. *The Way of Jesus Christ: Christology in Messianic Dimensions*. Minneapolis: Fortress, 1993.

Niles, Damayanthi. *Doing Theology with Humility, Generosity, and Wonder*. Minneapolis: Fortress, 2020.

Pearse, Mark Guy. *The British Friend* 1.1 (January 1892) 15. https://books.google.com/books?id=vDMrAAAAYAAJ&pg=PA14&source=gbs_toc_r&cad=2#v=onepage&q=remember&f=false.

Riley, Cole Arthur. *This Here Flesh: Spirituality, Liberation, and the Stories that Make Us*. New York: Convergent, 2023.

Rohr, Richard. *Everything Belongs: The Gift of Contemplative Prayer*. Chestnut Ridge, NY: Crossroad, 2003.

Starr, Mirabai. *Julian of Norwich: The Showings: Uncovering the Face of the Feminine in Revelations of Divine Love*. Charlottesville, VA: Hampton Roads, 2022.

Tanner, Kenneth. "Made Well." *The Human God*, February 24, 2025. https://kennethtanner.substack.com/p/made-well.

Bibliography

Tippett, Krista. "1,107: Kate Bowler—On Being in a Body." Produced by On Being Studios. *On Being*. September 21, 2023. Podcast, MP3 audio, 42:16–43:14. https://onbeing.org/programs/kate-bowler-on-being-in-a-body/.

———. "1,129: Christine Runyan—On Healing Our Distressed Nervous Systems." Produced by On Being Studios. *On Being*. May 30, 2024. Podcast, MP3 audio, 04:31–05:14, 14:43–17:34. https://onbeing.org/programs/christine-runyan-on-healing-our-distressed-nervous-systems.

Toolan, David. *At Home in the Cosmos*. Maryknoll, NY: Orbis, 2003.

Van der Kolk, Bessel. *The Body Keeps the Score: Brain, Mind, and Body in the Healing of Trauma*. New York: Penguin, 2015.

Woodley, Randy. *Indigenous Theology and the Western Worldview: A Decolonized Approach to Christian Doctrine*. Grand Rapids: Baker Academic, 2022.

www.ingramcontent.com/pod-product-compliance
Lightning Source LLC
Chambersburg PA
CBHW071443160426
43195CB00013B/2017